Falling Apart
-or-
Coming Together

To George + Marlene —
May God bless you
+ continue to use you
in very special ways!
Hugs!
Lois Johnson
James 1:2-4, 12

Falling Apart
-or-
Coming Together

How You Can Experience the Faithfulness of God

Lois Walfrid Johnson

AUGSBURG Publishing House • Minneapolis

FALLING APART OR COMING TOGETHER
How You Can Experience the Faithfulness of God

Scripture quotations unless otherwise noted are from the Holy Bible: New International Version. Copyright 1978 by the New York International Bible Society. Used by permission of Zondervan Bible Publishers.

Library of Congress Cataloging in Publication Data

Johnson, Lois Walfrid.
   Falling Apart or Coming Together.

   Includes bibliographical references.
   1. Christian life—1960-   . I. Title.
BV4501.2.J555 1984   248.4   83-72112
ISBN 0-8066-2056-0 (pbk.)

Manufactured in the U.S.A.   APH 10-2208

2   3   4   5   6   7   8   9   0   1   2   3   4   5   6   7   8   9

To Roland, Merriam, Leland, and Norma

because you know that the testing
of your faith develops perseverance

James 1:3

Contents

Preface

In recent years I have become increasingly conscious of the effects of prolonged emotional turmoil on physical well-being. Yet few, if any of us, can exist without at some time feeling overwhelmed. You and I live in a world perilously close to the edge of a chasm—a chasm filled with the jagged rocks of many forms of possible ruin. Reasons for anxiety, guilt, rejection, depression, and hopelessness abound.

What happens if we bottle up our negative feelings for a long period of time? What if we allow them to remain like a neglected pot of stew, gaining heat, and eventually boiling over? Will our emotional condition affect whatever part of our body is weakest? Dr. Keith Sehnert, author of *Stress/Unstress*, says, "Protracted wear and tear can affect any of the body's organs or systems."

At times I am amazed at the power of a human being to take one onslaught after another without becoming physically ill. But on the other hand, I seldom pray for the physical health of someone without becoming aware that they first need prayer for inner peace. I clearly remember the emotional circles in which I traveled for years before being diagnosed with cancer. That knowledge encourages me to do something about the new situations confronting me daily.

But the question returns. Even as we recognize our personal need, can you and I experience spiritual and emotional peace? Often life seems like a jigsaw puzzle. We try to shape a beautiful picture, but discover our best is not enough. Only the Lord holds the overall strategy by which we come together. Can God give us a balanced awareness of and involvement in the world, yet also joy and the ability to endure when needed?

Margaret Truman writes, "Courage does not have to be constant, but I would like to see it become contagious." So would I, beginning with me. One day I realized that adversity forces us one way or another. Some people become animals. Others face the very worst and become their very best.

I asked myself: How can I cope with the feelings and problems that are often part of a stress-filled world? Why does one person knuckle under and another become stronger in periods of darkness? What qualities does God instill in those average people who become overcomers—quiet, often unacknowledged heroes or heroines—who show us that love, strength, and valor are still possible?

I knew that if I accepted the challenge of such questions, I would be called to put aside easy Christianity. The only faith strong enough for these times dwells in those persons prepared to follow unconditionally, ready to lay down their lives for Jesus Christ.

Yet deep within me a resolve formed. I wanted to be one of those who remain faithful, regardless of the cost. I felt sure I wasn't made of that kind of stuff. But what would happen if I turned over to God every part of my being—if I accepted Christ's challenge to see the close of the age as being like the days of Noah—days of preparation? What if I were willing to be spiritually, emotionally, and physically prepared by the Holy Spirit?

So began my search—a search that has not yet ended, for there are no easy answers. As a result, writing this book seemed an overwhelming task. But at the point where I wanted to turn and run, I remembered a prayer. Long ago I offered it as I entered the hospital for what proved to be a mastectomy. In thinking about all that might lie ahead, I asked, "Jesus, don't allow me at any time to feel separated from the sense of your presence."

I offer the possibility of that prayer to you in whatever you presently face. If you sense you are falling apart, may the presence of the Lord Jesus Christ enable you to come together. As you read, ask the Holy Spirit to bring these pages alive, to give you the needed thought at just the right time— a thought for your own life, a thought to encourage others.

In his faithfulness God will not fail you.

1 *In a world that is going to pieces we live out the choice:*

Are We Falling Apart or Coming Together?

As I prayed one morning, I saw Jesus in a new way. Staff in hand, hair and robes flowing out behind him, he moved in great strides across a plateau rimmed by sharp, jagged peaks. In my mind's eye I started after him, but even though the ground was level, I could not keep up.

Without slowing his pace and seemingly without effort, he climbed a steep mountain path, reached the crest, and went down the other side to a valley of lush, green grass. I kept running, trying to catch him, never seeming able to do so.

Many times before, I had been comforted by thinking of Christ as the Good Shepherd who goes ahead. This was different. Though I tried to hurry, I kept falling back. Afraid I'd lose sight of him, I cried out, "Lord, don't leave me behind! Don't leave me! I want to walk *with* you—not always be running after you, unable to keep up."

He turned around, and I sensed his grieved, small voice: "My child, you *are* lagging behind. I desire to do a new thing in your life, and you are not allowing me to do so."

I fell to my knees, asking forgiveness. I realized I had

reached a plateau in my spiritual walk, staying there instead of going ahead. Each time I resisted his growth, I hindered his power in the circumstances I faced. Pebbles in my shoes kept me from following in confidence and victory.

In subsequent weeks the Holy Spirit made me aware of the variety of ways in which I persisted in holding back. Some of those areas applied to me specifically; others were common problems in the body of Christ and the world. All around me—locally, nationally, and internationally—I discovered reasons to fall apart. Yet I longed for the ability to see each threat as an opportunity to experience God's faithfulness and power. I wanted to take the offensive, doing battle against reasons for anxiety and defeat, instead of simply waiting for the next attack.

I knew I could do nothing by myself. Yet as I thought about the situation, I decided to ask God to increase in me four qualities that would help me face difficult circumstances.

One sentence kept pounding its way into my consciousness: "Grow up in every way into him who is the head, into Christ" (Eph. 4:15 RSV). In common with many people, the first quality I needed was *a willingness to grow*. Each time I refused, I lacked the power necessary for living joyfully.

Alan Langstaff, founder of Vision Ministries, points out the difference between openness to growth and commitment to growth. Openness, says Langstaff, is a passive position: "As circumstances come in to your life you just put up sail and go with them." By contrast, he made an unlimited commitment to growth: "Consider the difference between the average person and a champion athlete. The latter *commits* himself to the discipline of physical development. Or look at the average student and the graduate of an advanced institution of learning. The graduate *committed* himself to using and developing his mind beyond meeting the basic requirements. The same applies to our personal walk with the Lord and our personal ministry before God." [1]

1. Newsletter, Vision Ministries (Route 1, Box 668, Cambridge, Minn. 55008), February 1982.

Once committed to growth, I needed a second quality to help me face difficult circumstances: *a God-given vision.* Solomon reminded us, "Where there is no vision, the people perish" (Prov. 29:18 KJV). Another version reads, "Where there is no prophecy the people cast off restraint" (RSV). In other words, without a vision they lose direction, even break loose from necessary inhibitions instead of living in balanced discipline.

I remember walking on a lonely country road. As I left the house, I turned on a spotlight, for there were no other lights for some distance. Then I headed away from the house, knowing that on one side was a woods of tall, deciduous trees; on the other, a stand of white pine 75 to 100 years old. Without a moon it was so dark that only the crunch of gravel beneath my feet told me I was still on the road.

After a time, I turned around and headed back toward the house. In that moment I could once again see. Everything fell into perspective: the mailbox, a path leading into the woods, the silhouette of branches against the sky. The light made the difference. I had direction even in a very dark world.

Spiritual vision begins as we know without doubt that we are Christians. Our sight increases as we live in the fullness of power that is the gift of the Holy Spirit. Beyond that, can any of us settle for a vision smaller than to be fully used by Jesus Christ?

Vision should also include our knowledge of the specific way God wants to use us. Within his call to be a missionary, Paul had a vision to go to the Gentiles. Our particular vision may be as unique as a fingerprint, but it should give a sense of movement toward something, or an ability to wait, even if we experience no results from our labor. In spite of that waiting, we receive the courage to pray against obstacles and work through hardships until we see the fulfillment of God's plan.

If we do not have that vision, that awareness of God's long view, we can ask for it. When the Spirit gives us a vision, we receive both direction and the farsightedness often needed to persevere in difficult situations.

In trying circumstances we also need a third quality: *expectancy*. For two years I walked without sight in a critical area of my life. The Holy Spirit taught me a spiritual pattern I later discovered in Watchman Nee's *The Spiritual Man*. My sense of expectancy has three parts: *He can. He will. He has.*

For most of us, it is no problem saying, "He can." As Creator of the universe, God can do anything! But what about the "he will" in our own difficult situation? If we feel unsure about what God wants to do, we need to go to Scripture, seeking specific direction. A leper came to Jesus, saying, "If you are willing, you can make me clean." Jesus replied, "I am willing. Be clean!" (Mark 1:40-41).

"He will" is the Spirit-given certainty or the scriptural promise we receive after honest searching and a desire to submit to God's leading. Through Scripture the Holy Spirit encourages us to pray with expectancy. Abraham became a father because he considered God faithful and able to keep a promise (Heb. 11:11).

In ancient Babylon Shadrach, Meschach, and Abednego stood before their king who held power over life or death. Refusing to bow to an image of gold, they said, "If we are thrown into the blazing furnace, the God we serve *is able* to save us from it, and *will* rescue us from your hand, O king" (Dan. 3:17).

He can. He will. Then, before experiencing the reality of God's protection, the young men went a step further: "But even if he does not, we want you to know, O king, that we will not serve your gods or worship the image of gold you have set up" (v. 18).

The faith of the young men held no doubt about who God is. Whatever happened, they believed in the Lord's faithfulness. In their world, as well as ours, God is sovereign.

Whenever we pray in the name of Jesus, you and I reenact the promise that he intercedes before the Father. He *has* entered on our behalf (Heb. 6:20). We may receive an awareness that "It is finished," or "It's taken care of." Often we sense "he has" in our spirit long before we see the reality of that for which we have asked.

Countless times I have seen miracles in answer to prayer. Yet when tempted to fall apart, I often need a fourth quality—the Spirit-empowered *ability to persevere,* to put one foot in front of another. James wrote, "Consider it pure joy, my brothers, whenever you face trials of many kinds, because you know that the testing of your faith develops perseverance" (1:2-3).

An elderly couple compared the depression of the 30s with the economic conditions of the 80s. "Sometimes water froze on the kitchen floor five feet away from the stove," said the wife. "Yes, but in some ways it's more difficult now," answered her husband. "Back then we weren't dependent on electricity. We cut our own wood, and when times were hard we just hunkered down."

It's that quality of "hunkering down" that all of us need spiritually. Growth, vision, and expectancy blend with stubbornness—not the stubbornness of insisting on our own way, but of recognizing the truth of Jesus Christ, taking a position, and being unwilling to settle for anything less.

Jesus calls us to walk, yes. But he also calls us to stand—to endure—to live without compromising that which is scriptural. Isaiah warned, "If you do not stand firm in your faith, you will not stand at all (Isa. 7:9). The writer of Hebrews encouraged, "We have come to share in Christ if we hold firmly till the end the confidence we had at first" (Heb. 3:14).

In all these things we are more than conquerors. Are we? Am I? Am I walking with Jesus Christ and standing firm when needed? Or am I running after him and yet powerless because I hold back parts of myself? Am I lagging behind?

You and I choose. If we choose to follow where God is leading us, the Holy Spirit makes good our decision. We discover God's faithfulness through all generations—a faithfulness established in heaven itself (Ps. 89:1-2). Instead of falling apart, we come together.

"The first is a solo act," said my friend Linda. "If we insist on doing something by ourselves, we *do* fall apart. But the second indicates a duet. We come together with God's help."

2 *When fear attacks, we stand firm in direct proportion to our personal dependence on God.*

Win over Fear!

The hands against the lighted dial said 2:00 A.M. Once more I rotated myself and my pillow, trying to squirm quietly rather than wake my husband. Yet I could not shut out of my mind the national and local newscasts. The events reported, the questions shouted, and the fears reinforced raised a specter. Not an obliging little one that quietly slid away the moment I turned off the TV, but a persistent foreboding that demanded my attention.

What if? The question could not be ignored. What if all those things we fear actually happened? In how many ways could our civilization, and I along with it, fall apart?

Today the world stands on tiptoe, always seeming about to take a plunge. Reasons for fear abound and are prominently advertised in every newspaper or newscast. Most of us push that fear to the back of our minds. Yet is that the way God wants you and me to live? With continual uneasiness?

A healthy fear is a warning, keeping us from going too close to the edge of a bluff. At times it is important to be afraid; in other moments it is devastating. A fear of failure causes us to study for an exam, but if we become too afraid we cannot concentrate. You and I need a balance between a fear*fulness* that can destroy us and a fear*less*ness that can destroy those around us.

Long ago the psalmist spoke about fears caused by circumstances beyond human control. Through God's power he had gone beyond those reasons to personal peace: "God is our refuge and strength, an ever present help in trouble. *Therefore* we will not fear, though the earth give way and the mountains fall into the heart of the sea, though its waters roar and foam and the mountains quake with their surging" (46:1–3).

How might we come to that same peace, winning over unhealthy forms of fear? The Lord is always faithful; learning to sense his faithfulness may involve a process:

1. Face the situation

Whenever a fear-producing situation confronts us, we choose between "fight and flight." On the morning my surgeon gave me a life-threatening diagnosis of cancer, I had to make a choice: Should I pretend I didn't hear what he was saying, or be honest about the possibilities and ask, "What will happen to me?"

As I thought about that question I had the biggest resource for coping with fear: knowing without doubt that I am a Christian. For all of us the battle against fear begins there. Even the worst can be conquered through eternal life.

By contrast, if we push aside reasons for fear, refusing to think about them, we encourage fear to multiply. A nurse working with cancer patients once told me she could do nothing to help such persons until they faced the fact that they had cancer. In the same way, if we deny what is going on around us, failing to face very real possibilities of catastrophic events, we shut ourselves off from God's help.

In response to a question put by his disciples, Christ gave several negative signs pointing to the end of the age: people coming falsely in his name, kingdoms rising against kingdoms, wars and rumors of wars, famines, earthquakes, persecution, and the increase of wickedness. Yet as we suffer under the multiplication of such signs, we remember his words: "See to it that you are not alarmed . . . he who stands firm to the end will be saved" (Matt. 24:6, 13).

Jesus would not give such instructions without providing the power to obey them. Moreover, he then offered a positive sign, apparently to encourage those who stand firm: "This gospel of the kingdom will be preached in the whole world as a testimony to all nations, and then the end will come" (v. 14).

2. Recognize coping as a process of growth

When we first face something that causes fear, there is a vulnerable time in which almost anything tips us off balance. I had to pray for protection from the stories people told me about other cancer patients. I thought about Job and how Satan asked God, "Have you not put a hedge around him and his household and everything he has?" (Job 1:10). As I considered those words, God stepped in. "Turn the stories over to me," the Spirit seemed to say. "Give me every fear. Ask for a hedge of protection encircling yourself, your husband, and your children. Through my Son I saved you from eternal death. I also want to save you from living in fear."

After a time of protection, I realized I needed to think more about the needs of others, and I offered a prayer based on Rom. 12:2: "Lord, transform me. Don't let me be molded by the fear I encounter. Renew my mind."

In reply, God showed me it is not the absence of fear that counts, but what I do regarding it—including praying immediately about any situation that makes me afraid. I needed to talk about my fear with a qualified person or loved one.

From that point, the Spirit led me to face a question: "What is the worst thing that could happen to me in connection with cancer?" I might die, as doctors had warned me. But was that truly the worst? What I really feared was the suffering I might experience before death.

Whoever we are, isn't the possibility of suffering one of our most overwhelming fears? Often people say, "Nuclear holocaust isn't my biggest fear. It's the possibility of living afterwards." We feel suffering is something we might not be able to handle. What if we lost control of our situation? Yet when Jesus said, "Lo, I am with you always, even to the end of the age," he promised to be with us, even if it involves suffering (Matt. 28:20 NAS). Who could better understand what it means to suffer? Who enables us to win, whatever the outcome?

3. Be still

The book of Proverbs tells us, "The fear of the Lord is the beginning of wisdom, and knowledge of the Holy One is understanding" (9:10).

When we fear God in this sense our reverence for him puts everything else in perspective. Without the Lord we have countless, *real* reasons for fear; with God we have none. The Spirit of Jesus within us becomes our resource for coping, however large the fear looms.

Only the Lord is big enough. We know God's character through a personal relationship and a thorough, ongoing study of Scripture. To deal with fear effectively, it is crucial to trust God speaking to us through Scripture. The Bible means what it says and gives positive steps for dealing with every situation.

Reasons for fear create a common denominator—our need for stillness. One young woman said, "When faced with my husband's unfaithfulness I was so upset that my thoughts went every direction. 'What's going to happen to our marriage? What about our future together? What will happen to me?' I couldn't even think. In that moment I had to remember, "Be still, and know that I am God" (Ps. 46:10).

She turned to *Streams in the Desert* and discovered encouragement to see difficulties, trials, and emergencies as opportunities for receiving new blessings and deliverances from God:

> Keep still, and stop your own restless working until He begins to work. Do nothing that He does not Himself command you to do. Give Him a chance to work, and He will surely do so; and the very trials that threatened to overcome you with discouragement and disaster, will become God's opportunity for the revelation of His grace and glory in your life, as you have never known him before.[1]

When we see God, we no longer see the reason for fear. In times of stillness we have the opportunity to recall Scripture and repeat the name of Jesus, praising him for who he is. The amount of power in our life will be in direct proportion to how much time we spend praising and worshiping the Lord.

4. Give space to the best

At 3:40 A.M. the phone rang, interrupting my sound sleep. Still in a fog, I ran for it, wondering what terrible thing had happened. At the other end of the line a low voice asked, "Do you mind that I'm calling this time of night?"

Thinking I was talking to our son away at college, I felt a fist of fear punching my stomach. "No, Kevin, I don't mind. What's the matter?"

"I'm lonesome," said the voice.

"Tell me about it," I answered, the fear within me growing. As I listened, questions rushed into my mind, as a river out of control. It was so unlike our 19-year-old. Usually self-sufficient, why was he lonely now, at the end of the school year? Was he ill with a high temperature? Had he been studying too hard?

By this time my husband Roy and our oldest son had quietly listened in on the extension. They joined me, looking disturbed. They, too, thought it was Kevin. My fear edged into panic as I asked, "Kevin, are you thinking ahead to next year when

---

1. A. B. Simpson, quoted by Mrs. Charles E. Cowan (Zondervan, 1965).

you'll be studying in Taiwan? Are you feeling lonesome about that?"

For a time he talked in generalities. Then without warning he began speaking obscenely. It seemed I had entered a nightmare in which walls closed around me. Feeling I could not bear the pain, I silently pleaded, "Oh, Lord, Lord, Lord. . . ."

A moment later the voice swore, using a word I had never heard Kevin speak. Instantly my head cleared. "Kevin, what's your middle initial?" I asked. "What's your favorite meal?" Like a tommy gun my questions came, as I sought beyond doubt to identify our son.

Apparently sensing the change in me, the caller hung up. Immediately my husband prodded, "Call Kevin." Grateful for the phone in his room, I dialed, and a sleepy voice answered. As Kevin spoke I caught the barely perceptible difference in voices. Without doubt I knew the caller had not been my son.

Out of his own faith Kevin offered comfort, yet as we said good-bye, I began to tremble. Roy and our oldest son prayed for me, asking God to cleanse my mind and bring peace. I crawled back into bed, but fear still raced through my being. How many more middle-of-the-night calls would I receive? Could I forget those terrible words? How often would I wonder about Kevin, especially when he was far across the Pacific? Was there a unique family way to identify a child away from home, even with a poor telephone connection?

Feeling tense in every muscle, I slowly unclenched my fingers. Years before God had shown me how to give space to the best, whatever the reason for fear. Out of long habit I entered that process:

• *Find the promise.* No two things can occupy the same space at the same time. When fear threatens, I tell God my specific need, asking, "What do you want me to know?" Repeatedly the Holy Spirit uses my daily reading of Scripture to make real a promise or passage. Often I memorize those verses around which the Spirit seems to put a holy spotlight. After the phone call, I remembered words I had learned some time before: "Let the beloved of the Lord rest secure in him,

24

for he shields him all day long, and the one the Lord loves rests between his shoulders" (Deut. 33:12).

• *Lay hold of the promise.* When the Holy Spirit illuminates a passage, I believe those words are a personal message to me. My spirit responds, "Lord, that verse is *for me.* Thank you!"

• *Pray the promise, affirming it.* I invite God to increase my faith by praying the words that have been highlighted. "Thank you, Lord, that I am loved by you, that you shield me, that you give me the ability to rest."

After the phone call, I recalled Scripture promises and repeated the name of Jesus. I focused on Christ, offering praise for who he is. The habit of praise welcomed the Spirit, and he flowed through my mind and emotions, dissipating fear as dew warmed by sunlight. Seldom had I sensed so strongly the Spirit's role as Comforter. Within a few days I no longer remembered the obscenities.

• *Kneel on the promise.* God's promises offer a rock in an ever-changing world. When fear returns in an area about which I have sought the Lord, I go back to the promise he illuminated. Kneeling on that rock, I tell him, "I believe your Word, even if I cannot yet see your work." I repeat his promise until I come to peace. At bedtime or in the middle of the night I drift into sleep with God's message as my last waking thought: "The beloved of the Lord rest secure in him."

5. *Recognize God's voice*

It seems part of the Lord's sovereignty that he is allowing an increase of end-time signs during an era when mass communication enables us to know daily what happens worldwide. Hearing of one crisis after another can be overwhelming, yet knowledge of current events assists us in recognizing those occurrences listed by Christ.

As we listened to reports of another crisis in the Mideast, I said to my husband, "That situation concerns me. It reminds me of what the Bible says."

Two hours later, as I again thought about the newscast, I

sensed the Spirit's direction in my thinking. I wondered, *Why am I afraid about events reminding me of Scripture? It should comfort me, because it means the Lord is in control.* The moment I started looking at the situation from that perspective, I sensed peace.

At the same time we should recognize God's warning. Amos reminds us, "Surely the Sovereign Lord does nothing without revealing his plan to his servants the prophets" (3:7). We need to hear the voice of God well enough to distinguish the difference between the warning that comes from him and the harassment that is of Satan. Satan gives glimpses of various possible catastrophes to cause paralyzing fear and the sense that the world is beyond hope. By contrast, God shows us such things to reveal the need for intercession, repentance, and spiritual, emotional, and physical preparation.

Always God loves us, but if we continually reject his best will for our lives, he does not force his protection on us. When we seek to live in the Lord's will, we discover our greatest protection—knowing God is with us. " 'Because he loves me,' says the Lord, 'I will rescue him; I will protect him, for he acknowledges my name. He will call upon me, and I will answer him; I will be with him in trouble, I will deliver him and honor him' " (Ps. 91:14-15).

Receiving God's protection does not mean he will always take us out of difficult circumstances, even though that is our preference. Through Isaiah God said he would take us *through* "the waters . . . the rivers . . . the fire" (43:2). Often God protects us in the midst of circumstances. After 23 years in Soviet prisons and Siberian labor camps, Jesuit priest Walter Ciszek wrote in *He Leadeth Me*, "No evil could touch me, ultimately, as long as God was with me."

Whenever we respond to God's leading, he releases us into peace and kingdom living: "By faith Noah, when warned about things not yet seen, in holy fear built an ark to save his family. By his faith he condemned the world and became heir of the righteousness that comes by faith" (Heb. 11:7).

6. Put your will on the side of faith

Faith is God-given, but we choose whether we allow the Spirit to enlarge our faith. When one young man named John Davidson travels on a plane, he asks the Lord for the opportunity to talk with someone. After such a prayer, he takes out his Bible and begins reading, for it helps people understand where he's coming from.

On one occasion the girl seated next to him immediately asked, "Oh, are you a Christian? I asked God to give me someone with whom I could talk."

She told John she was afraid to fly and sought her loving heavenly Father for Christian fellowship. Not only had she faced her fear; she had requested specific help in getting beyond it.

"Fear," says John, "can make you ineffective because you're bound up. Or it can cause you to become motivated." He tries to use fear as a motivating force, knowing that if he is led by God to go through the difficult rather than the easy, it will build something into him as a person: "The more you take on hard things, the more you develop as a Christian." Through God's grace he passes through the smokescreen of insecurity, winning over fear, to discover what God has on the other side.

When we think about the future, we may be afraid to voice a secret fear: "Can I trust God? Is the Lord big enough to handle even *my* circumstances?"

After his years in Soviet prisons and labor camps, Walter Ciszek considered what it means to come to an attitude of total trust in God: "He was asking a complete gift of self, nothing held back. It demanded absolute faith: faith in God's existence, in his providence, in his concern for the minutest detail, in his power to sustain me, and in his love protecting me. It meant losing the last hidden doubt, the ultimate fear that God will not be there to bear you up" (*He Leadeth Me,* p. 84).

We lose that hidden doubt, that ultimate fear, in the day-to-day experience of God's presence. The greater our reason for fear, the more deeply we realize a situation goes beyond us and must be held by God. We stand firm in direct proportion to our personal dependence on him.

Emotions come unbidden, whether we want them or not. Yet God created us with the ability to make choices. Then he gave the Holy Spirit to help us make the right ones. When we put our will on the side of faith, we say in essence, "I believe God is a person who wants me to walk ahead boldly, because he leads me into whatever future I have."

Paul wrote, "God hath not given us the spirit of fear; but of power, and of love, and of a sound mind" (2 Tim. 1:7 KJV). We know also that "Perfect love casts out fear" (1 John 4:18 RSV). To the degree that we allow the Spirit's love to enter our inner spirit, we will not know fear. Love is stronger. To the extent that we fill ourselves with his promises, we learn that reasons for fear can be overcome, not by our own capabilities, but by God's. Our attitude becomes that of the psalmist: "I trust in you, O Lord; I say, 'You are my God.' My times are in your hands" (31:14-15).

Splashing in her Saturday night bath, five-year-old Stacy hummed as her father supervised. Suddenly she said, "I wonder when the world is going to end." Without waiting for his reply, she continued, "I suppose it will end whenever God wants it to. . . ."

After thinking a moment she added, "Then God will make it all over again."

In the extremity of our greatest need, we go to a world made by God, our refuge and strength. Though the earth give way, we *will not fear*. As the psalmist said, "The Lord Almighty is with us; the God of Jacob is our fortress."

*Whenever we seek God honestly,
being willing to listen, we find him
ready to speak.*

You Can Hear
the Voice of God

You're confused, lacking direction, or hurting, needing comfort.
You're anxious, filled with fear, or wondering if your prayers
are being heard.

Perhaps you're even saying, "I'm not sure if it's the Lord
speaking or just me making things up. How can I *know* if I'm
hearing him?"

For one or all of these reasons, you need to recognize God's
voice and hear him say, "This is the way; walk in it" (Isa.
30:21).

Long ago, Jonathan lived in a confusing situation. His father,
King Saul, wanted to kill his best friend, David. Jonathan knew
that someday David would gain the throne which seemingly
should have been his. How could he be loyal both to his
father and David? Holding the power of life or death, he stood
between the two.

What could have been a terrible situation, tearing Jonathan
into a thousand shreds, seemed no problem for him. Why?
What enabled him to live, apparently having no false guilt or

jealousy, but instead an amazing loyalty to David? As one young man pointed out, Jonathan knew the mind of the Lord. Out of that, he interceded for David.

Knowing the mind of God is another way of saying that Jonathan heard God's voice and sensed his will. The more difficult our situation, the more desperately every one of us needs to know God's presence and leading.

Few of us believe we never make a mistake in understanding the Lord's wishes. Yet, as we walk in faith, we learn to recognize the ways in which God speaks. We realize also that he will correct us if we take a wrong turn. Jesus described himself as the Good Shepherd, saying the sheep follow because they know his voice. It *is* possible for us to do the same.

In his faithfulness God offers several means through which we hear his voice, and then provides corresponding safeguards. When we sense the Lord's will, these guidelines and safeguards flow together, confirming one another.

Scripture

Cheri mentioned an important step in battling confusion: "When I'm faced by something new, or frightening, or hard to decide, I try to get alone with the Lord before talking with other people."

When we are still before the Lord, we give him the opportunity to speak to us. If we are consistent readers of Scripture, we learn to recognize the Holy Spirit's illumination when he gives leading after prayer about a specific need. It's as though a verse or passage jumps off the page under a divine spotlight. The Spirit also spotlights groups of verses in areas for which we need understanding. Over a period of time he may arrange our personal schooling by showing us what Scripture says about various topics such as forgiveness, prayer, or perseverance.

If we're serious about hearing God's voice, it's easy to think, "What if I miss what he is trying to tell me?" When we are honest in our seeking, the Holy Spirit speaks, whether we read from the Old Testament or the New. The Spirit also uses more than one means of guidance, as though saying, "I won't let you miss what I want you to know." You may visit a church across the country, but the Holy Spirit uses the pastor to say what you've already heard in your own place of worship. Sometimes it's a heartwarming reassurance to realize that everyone is suddenly using the same verse of Scripture.

You and I receive help from the Lord in direct proportion to how dependent we are on him. To reach that dependence we need to believe that God means what he says. Through the Bible he offers a prescription for living. Those things forbidden in the Word of God are forbidden, those regarded holy *are* holy.

When we recognize the authority of Scripture, we believe God does not lie, but leads in ways consistent with his character (Heb. 6:17-20). Out of that comes our first safeguard: *All guidance, encouragement, or answers to prayer should be found in Scripture or be consistent with the overall body of truth taught there.*

There's an important question for all of us: "What kind of passage is the Holy Spirit making real to me?" When we know that, we have a solid beginning for hearing his voice in both specific and long-term ways.

Inward assurance

When seeking God's will, you may receive scriptural guidance first. On other occasions, you may have an inward assurance that is then confirmed through Scripture. Many Christians describe this inward leading in the way Elijah did—as a still, small voice from deep within.

Through that voice, God shows his concern for us and for the details of our life. In communist countries the Holy Spirit has led Christians step-by-step to the house of strangers. There they found refuge with other Christians. During times of persecution, the Spirit has also set places and hours of meeting. Every believer in the group has been present.

Since it's possible to hear from both God and Satan, it's important to remember a safeguard—the prayer, *"Lord, if this thought is of you, increase it; if not, remove it."*

Another means of assurance is a deep inner knowing. Think of Paul saying, "I *know* whom I have believed." When Christians are asked, "Explain what you mean by knowing," they often reply, "I can't describe it; I just *know.*"

Many Christians also receive a nudging to do something or leave it undone. Scripture doesn't tell us why Mary went to visit Elizabeth, but I suspect the Holy Spirit gave her an "I-ought-to" feeling. She was blessed by her cousin's response.

In connection with these means of inward assurance, God sometimes gives a sense of urgency that it is time to act. For example, you might be led to mow the lawn of an elderly neighbor, or call a friend who, without your knowledge, has just received bad news. If this urgency is God-given, you generally will not know peace until you act.

Our ability to hear the Spirit's voice and recognize his leading grows with experience. When you wonder about doing something, ask the question, *"Am I being led to do something that is consistent with Christ's love for all people?"* An action not in keeping with God's command to love one another is not his leading.

God also gives inward assurance through dreams or visions. Both John and Peter received visions while praying. As a prisoner on the island of Patmos, John wrote, "The Spirit took control of me, and I heard a loud voice, that sounded like a trumpet, speaking behind me. It said, 'Write down what you see . . .'" (Rev. 1:10-11 TEV). The vision that followed became the book of Revelation. From Peter's vision on the rooftop came the giving of the gospel to the Gentiles (Acts 10:9—11:18).

Soon after the birth of Christ, Joseph was warned in a dream to take the baby and Mary to Egypt. So great was the urgency of the message that Joseph did not wait for morning, but acted immediately. In a similar way, a Christian I know received a dream so powerful that she remembered every detail. Not long after, she again experienced almost the identical dream. Then, in her morning devotions, the Spirit made real the words of Joseph of Egypt: "The doubling of Pharaoh's dream means that the thing is fixed by God, and God will shortly bring it to pass" (Gen. 41:32 RSV).

Within a three-week period, from people unknown to each other and living far apart, I heard two other versions of the same dream. In each the symbol was different, but the identical message occurred: a warning of difficult times, but "Keep your eyes on the Lord, and he will take you through."

I believe these people received a godly message, but dreams can also spring from a meal of fatty foods, onion rings, and chocolate cake. For that reason, we need to observe a safeguard: *If you wonder about a dream being worthy of attention, ask the Lord if it is of him, and if so, to confirm it in another way.* Unless you hear as well and as urgently as the two Josephs, wait for that confirmation before making a life-changing decision.

Through Scripture and inward assurance, we often form a belief of what God wants. Then he may use the following means to strengthen that sense of guidance:

Righteous counsel

Solomon said, "In the multitude of counsellors there is safety" (Prov. 11:14 KJV), but it depends who those counselors are. A large group of friends may encourage us to do something resulting in lifelong grief. Therefore, our counselors should be mature in the Christian faith and have insight about how God deals with his people.

If counseling runs contrary to biblical truth, it might be time to turn on your discernment button. You also need someone who understands God's long-term leading in your life. When Jesus told the disciples that he needed to go to Jerusalem to suffer and die, Peter lacked perception about Christ's earthly mission: "Oh, no, Lord, surely that won't happen to you."

When seeking counsel about something important, you might consider another safeguard: *Ask God for counselors who see your situation from God's viewpoint, not just their own.* Think about their counsel, asking yourself:

- Do I sense peace about following the ideas suggested?
- Does their counsel ultimately bring life? (Even though initially I may not want to forgive someone, for instance.)
- Is their counsel consistent with the principles of Scripture?
- Is it consistent with God's overall dealing in my life?

At the same time, consider another safeguard: *"Am I willing to talk this over with the right person?"* If not, ask yourself: "What am I ashamed of? What am I trying to hide? What am I uneasy about?"

Peace or uneasiness

One university tells its students: "If you can't make up your mind about a major, declare one, and start out in it. It's better to change than to remain undecided." No doubt they've seen students remain undecided for years.

One of my friends pointed out a test of peace offering similar guidance. It should not be used on a decision such as marriage, where it's important to know without a doubt whether or not to go ahead. But it might be helpful in such decisions as choosing a college or vocation, or selling a home.

First, define the decision you need to make. Narrow it down to two clear-cut choices, A and B. Write down those choices. List first the good points, then the disadvantages under each. Then pray something like this: "Lord, to the best of my ability I believe you want me to take choice A. That's what I plan to do." Think that way for a week. *If you sense peace* and the timing is right, it will probably be all right for you to go ahead.

If, instead, you *lack* peace, go back to the place where you believe you made a wrong decision. Tell the Lord, "I'm going to take choice B instead." If you sense peace in that, continue in the assurance that you understand his will.

Paul wrote, "The peace that Christ gives is to guide you in the decisions you make . . ." (Col. 3:15 TEV). This is an inward sense that comes in spite of circumstances and offers another safeguard: *If you lack peace, do not go ahead with doing something.*

Confirming circumstances

Think of how God announced the birth of his son: "And this shall be a sign unto you; Ye shall find the babe wrapped in swaddling clothes, lying in a manger" (Luke 2:12 KJV). God gives signs to encourage faith, but he doesn't want you so busy looking for them that you fail to follow the road he quietly paves. Neither does he want you to use signs as a way of testing him, or, by contrast, to refuse his signs out of unbelief. Instead, when you have done your best to listen for the Spirit's guidance and discern his will, God will bless your honest request for help.[1] It is not a lack of faith to ask him to confirm his leading.

Signs might involve circumstances that are open doors. Not every opportunity is an "open door." High school graduates, for instance, may have such a variety of opportunities that a choice seems overwhelming. Instead, an open door follows specific prayer in an area so that things fall into place in a step-by-step pattern. These circumstances are arranged so perfectly that only God could be responsible. As the psalmist said, "The steps of a good man are ordered by the Lord" (37:23 KJV). When we sense that ordering, we need to go as far ahead as he directs. Otherwise, our leading may stop.

Closed doors may offer even more of a clear-cut direction. When Paul wanted to go into Asia, the Spirit of Jesus said no (Acts 16:6-7). Yet the apparent failure became eventual success when Paul began missionary work in Europe.

Such closed doors are different from situations when you need to continue in intercessory prayer. You sense that God has given a no, and that you shouldn't keep knocking.

At times the Spirit uses the words of others as a confirming

---

1. See Matt. 16:1; Exod. 17:1-7; Isa. 7:11-14; 2 Kings 18:5-7; 19:14-19, 29-34; 20:1-11 for examples.

circumstance. I feel best about that kind of situation when I have prayed about something and the person who speaks to me knows nothing about my specific prayer for God's guidance.

A friend may say, "The Lord told me I should tell you this." If you are not sure whether to believe someone's comment, remember this safeguard: *If God wants you to know something, he normally reveals it to you first, often through Scripture, then uses other persons or situations to confirm your understanding.*

Paul knew the danger of going to Jerusalem, yet felt compelled by the Spirit (Acts 20:22-23). Later, the prophet Agabus took Paul's belt, used it to tie his own hands and feet, and confirmed what Paul already sensed: "The Holy Spirit says, 'In this way the Jews of Jerusalem will bind the owner of this belt and will hand him over to the Gentiles.'" Paul was being prepared for his victorious testimony as a prisoner (21:4, 10-14).

God's provision

Through confirming circumstances and provision, the Lord gives both a promise and a safeguard: *If God wants you to do something, there will be a way to do it.*

Hudson Taylor said, "Where God guides, God provides. . . . God's work done in God's time, in God's way, will never lack God's provision." Sometimes money arrives in one lump sum, the correct amount to the penny. On other occasions, it comes a piece here, a piece there, as though God wants to test our faith. Occasionally I have been grateful there hasn't been the money for what I wanted to do. I would have run ahead of God's plan.

A question comes to each of us who wants to hear God's voice. That question is one you and I cannot ask lightly, but out of the times in which we live. As you walk daily in Christ's footsteps, the Holy Spirit will gradually unfold the answer, enabling you to live in faith. " 'For I know the plans I have for you,' declares the Lord, 'plans to prosper you and not to harm you, plans to give you hope and a future. Then you will call upon me and come and pray to me, and I will listen to you' " (Jer. 29:11-12).

And so we ask the question: "Lord, what are you saying to me—as an individual, as part of a family, as a member of the body of Christ—concerning the time ahead?" Out of that we have the opportunity to pray, "Lord, help me to be your person, in your place, in your time."

4 *Whenever we worry we say, "Lord, you're not going to take care of me." He wants to help us. . . .*

Escape the Prison of Worry

A Christian businessman was arrested for a crime he did not commit. "They snapped on handcuffs, took me to the station, and locked me into a small, dirty cell," he said. "All it had was an old iron cot.

"I wanted to get angry and depressed, but I just couldn't. I wanted to worry about getting out. Instead, I lay down on the cot and started to pray. Within 10 seconds I was sleeping like a baby. At 8:30 the next morning the police had to wake me for breakfast. I was sore from the iron bar that pressed against my back all night, but I felt rested in a way I hadn't for a long time."

Every one of us—young or old, male or female—experiences reasons for worry so great that we wonder if we can even pray, let alone receive an answer. Those who talk the most are not always the most serious worriers. You and I may be strong, silent types, never mentioning what really bothers us—outwardly calm, but tense on the inside.

Or, our worrying may take the form of procrastination. We feel inadequate, unable to begin a task. Worry also makes itself known through rebellion, as children who worry about a parent's situation sometimes illustrate.

When anxiety makes us feel we are falling apart, how can we experience God's faithfulness, even his peace in spite of circumstances? Let's consider seven means through which he helps us escape the prison of worry:

1. Receive insight

If something needs to be done, we get rid of worry only by taking small, bite-size chunks out of a necessary task. Usually it helps to begin in the area that seems easiest, achieve a small measure of success there, then go on to the rest of the work.

Worry is a contagious disease that seems to run in families. Unless an individual receives insight, consciously seeking to break the pattern, worry can be a habit passed from one generation to another. We teach our children to meet life in the way *we* respond, whether that is through worry or trust.

William Barclay writes, "God's rescuing power is not something to be played and experimented with, it is something to be quietly trusted in the life of every day." If you are not a Christian, you *should* worry. You do not have the promise of eternal life, nor the promise of provision for your need. But if you are a Christian, it is a different matter.

Whenever we worry, we say, "Lord, you're not going to take care of me," or, "You're not going to watch over my loved ones." Instead of relying on God, we trust in our own ability to control our life or that of someone else. Our release from the prison of worry begins when we recognize and confess anxiety for what it is—the sin of unbelief.

Anxiety hinders the Lord's work in a life. He knows far in advance what is going to happen to us, and has it all planned out, subject to our free will. Yet worry puts up steel bars, locking in what we allow him to do. God will not violate free will, and our hanging on to a concern may hinder him from giving us the best. Out of her experience of suffering in a Nazi concentration camp, Corrie ten Boom told John Dawson and his friends, "Don't wrestle . . . nestle."

39

2. *Make a choice*

You and I indicate preferences every day. What should I eat for dinner? What clothing should I buy? Should I do this work now or later? Each time we make a choice, we consider what is best for us. Then we choose with our will, believing we know the difference between good and evil, or good and best.

Worry involves the same kind of choice. Should we snap handcuffs on our reason for concern? Or bring the situation before the Lord, allowing him to deal with it? As one person said, "If you worry, why pray? If you pray, why worry?"

The single biggest secret in dealing with worry involves seeking the Lord until we receive his specific promise about that area of concern. (See the four steps on pp. 24-25). Then, if we rely on the Holy Spirit, he gives us the power to live by that promise. As David said, "Some trust in chariots and some in horses, but we trust in the name of the Lord our God. They are brought to their knees and fall, but we rise up and stand firm" (Ps. 20:7-8).

When our son Kevin was 16 years old, he wanted to serve with a short-term missionary group for a summer in Venezuela. I asked, "Tell me the leading God has given you." I needed to know whether he would be living within the will of the Lord.

Kevin showed us a number of verses he had received, including one that spoke specifically to his giving a summer without earning money: "You have received without paying, so give without being paid" (Matt. 10:8 TEV). As a family we joined in asking that his inward leading be confirmed in an outward way—that he receive the support needed in order to go.

While Kevin was in Venezuela, we had several reasons to feel concerned, including a five-week delay in mail, and one of the worst hurricanes of the century whipping through that area. Each time worry threatened, I tried to remember the leading he had received. Through those verses, the Holy Spirit gave me the faith to believe that whatever happened— good or bad—Kevin lived within the Lord's care.

3. Keep it simple

I have experienced countless times in which my reason for worry has been so desperate that I asked, "Jesus, pray for me," or, "Holy Spirit, pray through me" (see Luke 22:32; John 17:20; Rom. 8:26). Whenever we pray, we have the privilege of making it simple. The Lord will hear and understand if we simply call out, "Help!"

There are many ways to describe what we need to do when praying about a matter causing worry. Someone may tell us, "Turn it over to the Lord." Scripture puts it, "Cast all your anxiety on him" (1 Peter 5:7). Or we may pray, "Lord, I give this whole thing to you." Essentially, these phrases mean the same thing. But you may wonder, "How do I do what they suggest?"

The best comparison might be what happens in gift giving. Imagine that I am putting all my reasons for worry in a box. I like those worries, or I *seem* to, because I keep thinking about them, as though they are something special. So I wrap them beautifully with lovely paper and a big red bow.

Then I have a choice. Am I going to keep that "gift" of worry, hugging it to myself, not allowing it to leave my life? Or am I going to hand it to the Lord? If I am willing, the Holy Spirit gives me the ability to give God a worrisome situation as it truly should be given—without taking it back.

4. Readjust your focus

Usually we worry about the "what ifs." What if this happens? What if that doesn't happen? Ultimately the question becomes, "What will happen to *me?*"

Ninety-nine percent of the time the thing that we worry about never occurs. Yet there are also situations when our anxiety concerning something draws the problem to us. A man who worries about getting an ulcer, but does nothing to change his stressful life-style, programs himself to get an ulcer.

At times, worry becomes a refusal to fight and pray against the threat of evil. If, instead, we allow the Holy Spirit to work, he takes the focus off our own self and puts it where it belongs—on God. In his faithfulness he brings us to realize *I can't, but he can.*

Isaiah spoke about that kind of focus: "Thou dost keep him in perfect peace, whose mind is stayed on thee, because he trusts in thee" (26:3 RSV). When our mind is stayed on God, it becomes steadfast, and a steadfast mind brings stability into our entire life.

The psalmist wrote, "I have set the Lord always before me. Because he is at my right hand, I will not be shaken." The result is interesting: *"Therefore* my heart is glad and my tongue rejoices; my body also will rest secure" (16:8-9).

Think of a common area of worry: our work. Too often it appears we are not conscientious unless we worry. We should do our best in any area of responsibility, but worry can hinder that best. In *The Christian's Secret of a Happy Life* Hannah Whitall Smith explains:

> If the work is His, the responsibility is His, also, and we have no room left for worrying about results. . . . The most effectual workers I know are those who do not feel the least care of anxiety about their work, but who commit it all to their dear Master, and, asking Him to guide them moment by moment in reference to it, trust Him implicitly for each moment's needed supplies of wisdom and strength (Revell, 1942; pp. 135-136).

Out of this understanding, I often pray, "Lord, the work is yours. The responsibility is also yours." I repeat that prayer each time I feel tension about deadlines or my ability to produce.

To give the Lord responsibility for our work does not mean we become careless in doing our part. Instead, we are freed for our best because we do not carry the weight.

5. *Learn to rest*

One individual told me, "If things are going well I worry because there's not anything to worry about. I feel sure something awful is going to happen."

Another person, a woman I know well, realized that something was missing in her life. She asked, "Why have I failed to grow in my Christian life as I should?"

She sought a straight answer, but I hesitated, not wanting to hurt her. Then I sensed the Spirit's quiet prodding: "You will stand between her and God if you refuse to give the answer." Quietly I responded, "I feel it is because you have not learned to rest." I meant, of course, that she needed to trust God.

Tears filled her eyes. "Lois, two other people have told me exactly the same thing."

We asked the Lord for more power in her prayer life and the ability to trust him. Months later, I learned how God had answered these requests. As we talked about her daughter, she remarked, "It's a situation in which I don't know what is best, but the Lord is helping me rest."

What does it mean to rest? I think of it as lying down on a bed. No one sleeps six inches above a mattress, held there by their ability to control a situation. We rest only if we allow our bodies to be supported by the bed.

So, too, with worry. God's love is the mattress. He desires to hold us. But if, out of habit, we continue to hold ourselves above the mattress of his love and staying power, we never rest.

Solomon said, "Trust in the Lord with all your heart and lean not on your own understanding" (Prov. 3:5). The way of the world is to depend on that which we understand or on those things which were created through human understanding. God expects us to believe that he knows what he is doing, even in times when we feel imprisoned by circumstances. He desires that we know everything we can about hearing his voice and recognizing his will. Beyond that, the Lord may call us to take radical leaps of faith because our trust is *in him.*

Learning to rest is not just a yearly, monthly, or even weekly project. To leave the bondage of worry behind, we need to trust God moment by moment. That need should keep us forever humble, for even the ability to rest is God-given. It requires the power of the Holy Spirit. God always takes the initiative in our lives and makes it possible for us to respond to him. If we do our part, we are enabled to live out the promise offered by the psalmist: "He who dwells in the shelter of the Most High will rest in the shadow of the Almighty. . . . He will cover you with his feathers, and under his wings you will find refuge; his faithfulness will be your shield and rampart" (91:1, 4).

6. Refuse readmittance

Martin Luther once said, "I have held many things in my hands, and I have lost them all; but whatever I have placed in God's hands, that I still possess."

If we pray, "Lord, I give the reason for my worry to you," we commit that situation to him. Whenever we commit something to a person, we give over custody of it for safekeeping. Out of the suffering of his imprisonment, Paul wrote, "I know whom I have believed, and am persuaded that he is able to keep that which I have committed unto him against that day" (2 Tim. 1:12 KJV).

If we allow him, Satan will return to bother us about those areas we've committed to the Lord. When something goes wrong, he even encourages us to think, "If I had worried more, it never would have happened." It doesn't work to argue with him. Our attempt to do so is our first step back into worry. But we can pray immediately, "Lord, that's committed to you." If necessary, I repeat those words until I sense peace.

7. Rechannel your energy

When evil attacks, we too often stay in the prison of worry, instead of grasping hold of the power the Lord can set loose. Or we think it impossible to hold back wickedness by praying for change through the power of the Holy Spirit.

Out of his experience with imprisonment, shipwreck, and escape from death, Paul told the Ephesians, "Pray in the Spirit on all occasions with all kinds of prayers and requests" (6:18). If we pray in the Spirit, we yield ourselves completely to him, and he prays through us. We experience God's faithfulness and a sense of oneness that brings us to peace.

Prayer is the most creative way I know to use energy that would be wasted in worry. In his faithfulness God gives us the privilege of seeing each reason to worry as an encouragement to pray. When my loved ones and I are separated by distance, I ask the Holy Spirit to remind me if they need additional prayer. I try to continue praying until I receive a release of peace—a feeling of "It's okay now." That sense may come as I see the answer, or before I see it.

As we grow in Christian maturity, we learn to recognize the difference between resting in faith or standing to meet a challenge. When formidable situations arise, we respond to them according to the habit we have formed in less difficult times. When we choose to pray, the Spirit of prayer releases us from prison.

The Truman Library at Independence, Missouri, displays a letter dictated to Olive Truman, wife of the vice president's cousin. Dated April 12, 1945, the day President Roosevelt died, it started as a neatly typed routine letter discussing family business. Then, across the bottom appears Truman's hurried scrawl: "I've really had a blow since this was dictated. But I'll have to meet it. Hope it won't cause the family too much trouble."

As Christians, we have the opportunity to go beyond even this admirable human feeling to a Spirit-given sense of faith that declares, "With God's help I *will* meet the challenge."

While a child, I liked to walk with my six-foot, two-and-a-half-inch father, though I found it hard to keep up. But then I learned to put my hand in his and take two of my biggest, half-running steps to one of his.

Whenever I need to trust, God always takes a bigger step than I think I can manage. Yet if I put my hand in his, he leads me from the prison of worry.

5 *The test of our faith comes*
when it enters practical areas.

Living under the Lord's Provision

We had driven for three days. Jammed into the backseat of our car, I buried my nose in a pamphlet dealing with prosperity. Soon I was lost in reading.

"Lois, are you seeing this?" my husband asked.

I looked up to squalor on both sides of the road: Tumble-down shacks on blocks to discourage termites; a porch leaning precariously, the support gone; tin roofs. I wondered if those shelters became boiling cauldrons in the summer sun.

It was not the first time I had seen poverty. Nor were those shacks the worst to be found. But they created a grieving within me. If I had the opportunity to talk with those people, how would I reconcile the great variety of Christian teachings concerning finances? Beyond that, what could I say to a Christian family struggling with unemployment and wondering why they are not prosperous?

The test of our faith comes when it enters practical areas. I needed to think through a scriptural view of finances. What *is* God's provision? How can it be real in my life? I asked the Holy Spirit to teach me in the following areas:

Prosperity and blessing

Often we use the word *prosperity* to mean only material abundance. In doing so, we severely limit God. The New American Standard Bible calls prosperity "a state of material or spiritual bountifulness." As we study Scripture, we see that prosperity frequently describes having success in what we do.

Consider Joseph's situation with Potiphar: "And the Lord was with Joseph, so he became a successful man." The word *successful* is footnoted "prosperous," and the next verse reinforces this: "Now his master saw that the Lord was with him and *how* the Lord caused all that he did to prosper in his hand" (Gen. 39:2-3 NAS).

The passage goes on to use the word *blessing*, suggesting something even greater than prosperity: "And it came about that from the time he [Potiphar] made him [Joseph] overseer in his house, and over all that he owned, the Lord blessed the Egyptian's house on account of Joseph; thus the Lord's blessing was upon all that he owned, in the house and in the field" (v. 5).

The New American Standard Bible describes *blessing* as "the gift of God's grace." We may mistakenly feel we deserve certain things; by definition we receive blessing because of God's gift to us. The Lord's blessings show a wide variety of ways he cares for his children: forgiveness, salvation, food, clothing, water, shelter, rain for harvest, long life, godly children, and peace rather than war.

God's conditions

Blessings such as forgiveness and salvation are always free— no strings attached. In other passages of Scripture having to do with discipleship or finances, God offers an "if/then" arrangement. If you, my people, do this, then I, your God, will do this.

You might think that results in bondage. Instead, with

understanding comes freedom, for the Holy Spirit gives the power for our part. Think about three passages, noticing the italicized condition, and then the blessing:

Malachi 3:7-11: God and Israel held a conversation. " '*Return to me,* and I will return to you,' says the Lord Almighty." "What's the matter?" asked Israel, and God responded, "You're robbing me in your tithes and offerings."

He didn't spare words: " 'You are under a curse—the whole nation of you—because you are robbing me. *Bring the whole tithe into the storehouse,* that there may be food in my house. *Test me in this,'* says the Lord Almighty, 'and see if I will not throw open the floodgates of heaven and pour out so much blessing that you will not have room enough for it. I will prevent pests from devouring your crops, and the vines in your fields will not cast their fruit.' "

2 Chronicles 7:13-14: "When I shut up the heavens so that there is no rain, or command locusts to devour the land or send a plague among my people, *if my people, who are called by my name, will humble themselves and pray and seek my face and turn from their wicked ways,* then will I hear from heaven and will forgive their sin and will heal their land."

Luke 6:38: "*Give,* and it will be given to you. A good measure, pressed down, shaken together and running over, will be poured into your lap. For *with the measure you use,* it will be measured to you."

The right motivation

Jesus assured us that our heavenly Father knows what we need (Matt. 6:32). Even in desperate days of unemployment we have that promise. Paul explained how to receive: "Don't worry about anything, but in all your prayers ask God for what you need, always asking him with a thankful heart" (Phil. 4:6 TEV). But too often our needs turn to greeds, and we forget to ask, "Where is my heart?" (Matt. 6:21).

James wrote, "When you ask, you do not receive, because you ask with wrong motives, that you may spend what you get on your pleasures" (4:3). Paul said, "Each man should give what he has decided in his heart to give, not reluctantly or under compulsion, for God loves a cheerful giver" (2 Cor. 9:7). Jesus reminded, "Seek first his kingdom and his righteousness, and all these things will be given to you as well" (Matt. 6:33). A friend of mine summed it up: "If we look to God for what he does, instead of who he is, we miss the point."

When we know the promises of prosperity and blessing, it is easy to begin making business deals, seeing what we can wheedle out of God. The Lord desires that our giving come out of an abandonment that says, "I love the giver, not just the gift."

This is not the abandonment of throwing away money without discernment. Nor is it wasting money God gives for needs, refusing to work, or failing to seek training because "The Lord will provide." Spiritual abandonment springs from the wellspring of love which tells Jesus Christ, "I prefer you to everything else." As Paul wrote, "I consider everything a loss compared to the surpassing greatness of knowing Christ Jesus my Lord, for whose sake I have lost all things" (Phil. 3:8).

A deeply committed person described that kind of abandonment: "I had received four days of solid scriptural teaching. When the offering basket arrived, I wanted to encourage those whom the Holy Spirit had used in my life. Yet there was a quality in my giving that went beyond that.

"Out of my love for God, I gave an amount which for me was very large. I gave, not thinking about what I would get back; I didn't expect anything in return. The gift was a sacrificial one, but my confidence was in God. Somehow he would meet the needs of my family *in spite of* my gift. Months later, God blessed us in a special way. I probably would have missed the correlation except for one thing: he multiplied the exact amount I gave, not by 100, but by the amount *he* chose." (The 100-fold passage in Mark 10:29-30 refers to those who leave home for the sake of Christ and the gospel. It also promises both persecutions and eternal life.)

The crucial question is: Do I love the Lord so much that it doesn't matter whether he blesses me materially? A secret of the kingdom lies in that abandonment. Instead of earthen dams we become rivers of living water — channels of God's blessing.

Provision through guidance

God also gives provision and blessing through the way he plans for believers. In times of worldwide economic tightening, most of us hone our expenses to the bone and find the only way to live is under the Lord's economy.

Many times that does not mean receiving an increase of income, although it may. If we seek God's direction—being willing to give first out of whatever we have—we discover that somehow money stretches far enough. Not only does the Lord remove our desire for unneeded luxuries, he can alter expenses by guarding us against costly breakdowns, showing us how to decrease or omit utility bills, and helping us stay well rather than be plagued with high medical bills.

The Holy Spirit may also lead us to ask for wisdom and foresight in practical areas. There was a time when the Spirit kept prodding me to buy extra blankets. Though I didn't see the need at that point, I did not sense peace until I followed his prompting. Two years later, when our earning capacity was stretched to the limit, we needed every one of those blankets for children away at college.

God protects us, sometimes even without our full understanding. In other instances he gives us a deeper understanding of the world in which we live. We may be led to ask, "Could I cope if my income were lost or seriously reduced, or if the world's living conditions changed drastically? What do I actually need? Water, food, shelter, clothing? Do I have alternative ways to deal with the demands of my particular climate, even in traumatic weather conditions? Could my family and I join resources with other Christians, sharing the same house if necessary?"

Or we may wonder, "In a time of severe economic tightening or collapse, what practical skill could I offer to help others? What necessary product would I provide?" When the Holy Spirit encouraged me to consider such questions, I tried to think of something for which I was especially equipped, such as a thorough knowledge of first aid. I also considered things others might not want to do. When I believed I had heard the Lord's guidance, I began learning and working in those areas. I pray that in time of need my resources and skills will fit together with those of other Christians, even as two hands clasp in friendship.

Obedience

To understand the importance of obedience in connection with blessing, we need to see the difference between the bondage of law (from which Christ has set us free) and responding to someone we love.

With the first, consider a human relationship in which you do something for another person because you feel you must. It's expected of you, so you do it. Relate that to tithing, and you may say, "Well, God tells me I should, so I will."

Then think of someone you love. You look forward to being with that individual. You think of thoughtful things to do, ways you can acknowledge your loved one as a special person. Likewise, our obedience to God's wishes should spring out of our great love for him. We know the delight of walking in his ways. Our giving flows out of that joy. A 22-year old described it by saying, "It's not hard doing something he gives me the desire to do."

For each of us obedience can mean a different thing. As I prayed about God's ongoing provision, the Holy Spirit highlighted Jeremiah 6:16: "This is what the Lord says: 'Stand at the crossroads and look; ask for the ancient paths, ask where the good way is, and walk in it, and you will find rest for your souls.'" For some time God taught me both the hardships and the blessings of those old ways: no credit cards, but no debt at the end of the month; a simpler life-style and new appreciation for lack of clutter; instead of edible junk, learning to cook with natural foods; time-honored neighborliness. It was not long before I knew rest in my soul.

A return to the old ways demands effort and a willingness to work, especially if God leads us to expand a garden, learn to sew, or heat with renewable resources. Generally it takes more time, and initially it may take investment. In my case, I believe God wanted me to be willing to work at any task that did not dishonor him. Eventually I saw his blessing—his gift of grace—in leading me into servanthood. But I also know that I can live very simply, even without electricity and running water.

Hebrews 11 shows us ordinary people who became God's faithful because they responded in the way he led: "By faith Abraham, when called to go to a place he would later receive as his inheritance, obeyed and went, even though he did not know where he was going" (v. 8). My friend Penny summarized the principle: "If I'm obedient to God, he will bless me." Then she cautioned, "But I have to let him decide whether the blessing is going to be emotional, spiritual, or material. God blessed Joseph, even in prison. I believe that was a spiritual reward."

Loosen the hold

In talking with a man from a third world country, I realized once again how far we have gone beyond real needs to culturally created ones. Worldwide, countless individuals hope only for a roof over their heads and a mat on the floor. What are our expectations?

For years tax laws have encouraged the accumulation, rather than avoidance, of debt. Frugality, responsibility, and the willingness to work have often seemed out of date. Propagators of the dream have taught, "Buy now, pay later. You deserve whatever you want."

We *need* to succeed in those things meaningful to us. But our ability to work, place of employment, and success are God-given. With humility I remember that all I am and all I have comes from God. I don't *deserve* anything.

In many Christians God is working a disenchantment with things. We need to live as described in the phrase used by Norma Spande—"holding loosely whatever we have." How can we loosen our hold, not in the sense of being careless, but with the knowledge that God means more? We do so only as we realize that all our security is in him.

Money itself is neither good nor evil. Yet if we lavish money on ourselves, we may grow increasingly hardened to spiritual truth. Christ told us: "Any of you who does not give up everything he has cannot be my disciple" (Luke 14:33). In teaching about his provision, God may take us through the process where we learn contentment in living with less.

In his book *My Utmost for His Highest* Oswald Chambers writes, "When God is beginning to be satisfied with us He will impoverish everything in the nature of fictitious wealth, until we learn that all our fresh springs are in Him." There have been times when the amount I received for my labor was so low that I wept. Out of those moments I learned to pray, "Jesus, you are my reward."

In these days God needs competent Christians able to accumulate and administrate large sums of money for mighty efforts in the kingdom. *Some* of those who ultimately have the greatest capacity of earning and giving might experience prolonged monetary testing—even unemployment.

When God gives a distaste for needless clutter, he may also inspire us with a vision for a work in which great amounts of money are needed. The two are not incompatible. If we are hearing the Lord about his use of us, and it requires no money, we won't be led to prevail in prayer for large sums. But if our vision entails a vast mission outreach, for instance, he will inspire us to ask, give us courage to wait for his timing, then bless us by providing.

That vision begins in the Spirit and must remain there so it does not lose balance. Often I have been so careful to ask only for our needs that I have in essence said to God, "Don't give us *more* than what we need." The Spirit corrected me, saying, "Ask big enough. Don't limit God." As one man said, "Whenever we deny the possibility of the miraculous we lessen the possibility of living in faith."

The miraculous

Some have flippantly said, "If I'm ever really in need, I'll trust God for a miracle." I'm not sure that I would be able to trust unless I knew him well before. With true need there often comes depression, and in depression, it's difficult to pray. Our ability to believe in hard times flows out of our habit in better days. If we believe God has the power to bless in any way he chooses, and if his blessing follows our abandonment to him, what then?

I had always thought the widow who fed Elijah was just a nice person. One day I noticed God's actual words: "I have *commanded* a widow in that place to supply you with food." When Elijah asked for bread and water, she acted in obedience to God. He gave her the ability to recognize Elijah. I doubt if she knew her food would multiply. But when she gave, it did (1 Kings 17:7-16).

God's provision through the miraculous shows some basic elements:

a. *There was a need.* In Ahab's reign there was no rain or dew for three years. God provided the continuous supply of the widow's oil and flour. When Jesus fed the 4000 and the 5000, he did so out of compassion (Matt. 14:14; 15:32).

b. *A thankful attitude.* On both occasions when Jesus fed the masses, he first offered a prayer of thanks (Matt. 14:19; 15:36).

c. *God the Father made more out of something.* He used everyday, available ingredients and multiplied them.

d. *An individual made a sacrifice, often a difficult one.*

Hiking along a northwoods river, my husband and I came upon a boy of eight or nine who had caught two very small fish. Proudly he held them up for our admiration and applause.

Immediately my thoughts flashed to the boy at the solitary place where 5000 were fed. Had he caught those fish himself?

How had he felt about giving them to an adult when, after all, they were his? Yet he offered his fish and bread to Jesus.

I've never known the provision of God's miracle to happen among scoffing individuals. But with children of every age, I have.

6 *Are we turning away*
from the Lord's best means for coping?

The Tornado?
Or the Storm Shelter?

No longer do we need statistics to recognize the problem. A heavy black cloud hovers above our nation and world. Lower and lower it sinks until heaviness seems to take even the air from our lungs. We sense that we are smothering.

And so we are. We face more than a storm cloud. As we watch, it turns into a funnel—a worldwide tornado affecting every one of us. Yet must you and I sit passively by, watching our country, our loved ones, and our own lives torn in every direction by destructive winds?

A tornado can drive even a straw into the trunk of a tree. So, too, are we people driven by one thought, "If it feels good, do it." The results are those of the whirlwind: rebellion; guilt; the sense of falling apart; inability to live with ourselves or others; a lack of meaningfulness and power; uneasiness instead of peace.

Always God waits with welcoming arms outstretched, pointing the way to his storm shelter. Yet if you and I say something that is sin is not sin, we grieve and offend his holiness. Not only do we lack the power to cope with all that is going on, we also refuse his grace.

The danger

Sin is anything that separates us from the love of God. It prevents or destroys our relationship with him and with others. It limits our effectiveness in prayer. In contrast with Satan, who condemns by naming "all those things," the Holy Spirit points out specific areas where we need to make confession. Sometimes he illuminates passages of Scripture; in other moments he shows us that sin can be any thought, act, or situation giving bondage.

Being controlled by the Holy Spirit brings joy and peace. But we can also be controlled by sin. Paul wrote, "Don't you know that when you offer yourselves to someone to obey him as slaves, you are slaves to the one whom you obey—whether you are slaves to sin, which leads to death, or to obedience, which leads to righteousness?" (Rom. 6:16). Often people seek help in dealing with sin by saying, "I know it's wrong because I can't think of anything else. It controls me."

Something that controls us becomes a god. Jeremiah's challenge offers a striking parallel for our day:

This is what the Lord Almighty, the God of Israel, says: Listen! I am going to bring a disaster on this place that will make the ears of everyone who hears of it tingle. For they have forsaken me and made this a place of foreign gods; they have burned sacrifices in it to gods that neither they nor their fathers nor the kings of Judah ever knew, and they have filled this place with the blood of the innocent (19:3-4).

What might our sacrifices to other gods involve? Over a period of many months, the Holy Spirit repeatedly brought one thought to mind: "I am the Lord your God. Have no other gods before me." Each time he made me aware of a specific area needing repentance.

Sometimes my worship of other gods involved things I had. Other times I idolized, through my longing for them, what I did not have. Or I clutched to myself memories of people who hurt me. I hung on to my lukewarm commitment, finding it comfortable. I rolled temptation around in my mouth, carefully tasting it, before spitting it out.

For each person the list is different, but idols involve anything you and I worship instead of the Lord God himself.

Jeremiah also challenges us about shedding innocent blood. We find many ways to do so—gossip, refusing to forgive, hurting a family by playing around with the husband or wife, abortion on demand. In the United States alone more lives have been destroyed than in all the ovens of Nazi Germany. In nearly every church I have visited in recent years at least one girl or woman has said, "I have had an abortion. I can't handle the guilt. Will you help me?" If you are one of those, read on to find out how God can give you peace.

There's another way in which I personally have drawn blood. One day the Holy Spirit spoke so sharply to me that I began to weep. In that terrible moment I realized how guilty I was of thinking myself better than others. Countless times I had looked down on those guilty of open sin, consciously or unconsciously thinking, "I have not sinned as they have."

John tells us, "If we claim to be without sin, we deceive ourselves and the truth is not in us" (1 John 1:8). A refusal to recognize sin and the fact that we are personally sinful cuts us off from the only solution—the love and grace of God.

Martin Luther said, "The Holy Spirit has called me through the gospel, enlightened me with his gifts, and sanctified and kept me in true faith." When the Spirit calls, he shows us our sin so that we may be freed from it. In Christ, God made provision for our imperfections.

To me it's a relief to acknowledge I am not perfect. For those desiring to do the same, Winkie Pratney suggests a prayer: "Show me the things I have done not just to hurt myself, not even just to hurt others. Show me the things I have done to hurt you."

"Yes, but . . ."

When God confronted Adam and Eve about their sin, Adam answered, "The woman you put here with me—she gave me some fruit from the tree, and I ate it."

God turned to Eve: "What is this you have done?" She replied, "The serpent deceived me, and I ate" (Gen. 3:12-13).

It's easy to rebel, and then, like Eve, put the blame on others. The Lord wants us to accept responsibility for our own part in any sin. Whenever we say, "Yes, but . . . ," we grieve him. Instead of living in his protection, we leave ourselves in the path of a tornado.

In Psalm 81 God declares, "If my people would but listen to me, if Israel would follow my ways, how quickly would I subdue their enemies and turn my hand against their foes!" (vv. 13-14). The door to blessing swings open on the oiled hinges of repentance and obedience.

Gerry refused to use the sin in her background as an excuse for her own problems. "There was much abuse in my family," she said. "I asked the Lord to cut any harmful bonds between me and my past. Then he gave healing, filling me with his love."

Does it sound too easy? Not when it's God's work.

We need to hate our sin, feel deeply sorry for it, and come to the Lord in brokenness. The Puritans prayed for the gift of tears which indicated deep repentance. They knew that "Godly sorrow brings repentance that leads to salvation and leaves no regret, but worldly sorrow brings death" (2 Cor. 7:10).

The remedy

Jesus did not compromise what is sin, but brought grace to every situation. Though he hated the sin, he loved the sinner: "All that the Father gives me will come to me, and whoever comes to me I will never drive away" (John 6:37).

After David took Bathsheba into his palace, he tried to hide her pregnancy by arranging for her husband's death. God used a prophet to bring conviction: "You are the man!" David had no doubt in his heart that he had committed both adultery and murder. Out of the depths he prayed, "Against you, you only, have I sinned" (Ps. 51:4).

Like David, you and I need to confess, or admit, our sin before the Lord, naming it specifically. Then we should renounce it in the name of Jesus, putting it away from us, and refusing to go back to it.

Paul described the process when he said to put off the old self and put on the new (Eph. 4:22-24). When we look to Jesus Christ, his Spirit gives the power to change—to repent—to *turn away from* sin and *turn to* righteousness.

To each of us Paul says, "God demonstrates his own love for us in this: While we were still sinners, Christ died for us" (Rom. 5:8). Our request can be very simple: "Jesus, I believe you died for my sins. I name them before you." (Do so.) "Please forgive and cleanse me."

God's grace is like a wave rolling in from the sea. When we confess our sin, he carries it out into the depths, never to be seen again. We are forgiven, not because we are strong swimmers, able to win each meet, but through yielding every part of our self to him.

Romans 1:18-32 warns of the gradual progression of sin, and specifically the sin of exchanging natural relations for unnatural ones. Paul points out that those who persistently refuse God's truth receive in themselves the penalty for their perversion. Eventually they become unable to discern right from wrong: "Since they did not think it worthwhile to retain the knowledge of God, he gave them over to a depraved mind, to do what ought not to be done."

For example, one young man, who repented and asked for God's grace to lead a godly, celibate life, described his struggle with homosexuality: "Regardless of how accepted you are in the lie of life, there is still something that comes in to tell you it is not right. The lie is that homosexuality is okay. Satan tells you, 'It's fine; go at it.' God says, 'No, I made you a heterosexual individual.' First, get rid of the lie, then get rid of the deceit and the problems like anger that build up against the world."

For this young man, and for all of us who recognize our own sin and repent, God promises, "If anyone is in Christ, he is a new creation; the old has gone, the new has come!" (2 Cor. 5:17). If you desire to be a new creation, consider the steps through which we turn from sin to joy:

1. When the Holy Spirit convicts, recognize sin as sin, acknowledging that you are personally sinful.

2. Confess, or admit, your specific sin, refusing to say, "Yes, but. . . ."

3. Be sorry for your sin.

4. Ask Jesus for forgiveness.

5. Receive *in faith* his love, forgiveness, and peace.

6. Through the power of the Holy Spirit turn from your sin, commit yourself to a new life.

Changing from overweight to a slender body involves a commitment to dieting. So, too, turning from sin to righteousness involves commitment. We tell Jesus that we mean business and desire the power of the Holy Spirit in order to be new persons. That commitment might be needed in two ways:

• If you have confessed your sin, but do not have the assurance that you are a Christian, pray, "Jesus, I believe you died for me. I ask you to be my Savior, and Lord over every area of my life. I commit myself totally to you. Thank you for salvation and eternal life beginning right now." Then read Rom. 10:9-13 and 1 John 5:11-15. John said, "I write these things to you who believe in the name of the Son of God so that you may *know* that you have eternal life" (v. 13).

• If you know without doubt that you are a Christian, you may want to pray something like this: "Lord, I commit myself to a changed life by the power of the Holy Spirit. Give me the ability to walk in ongoing repentance, living in your righteousness."

You are then ready for a final step:

7. Cooperate with the Holy Spirit to change old habits. Ask God to heal your wounds.

After receiving forgiveness, we sometimes need help in dealing with ingrained patterns of living such as worry, self-pity, or unforgiveness. In a similar way, Outpost, a ministry in St. Paul, Minnesota, works with homosexuals who desire to be set free. To do so, they confess homosexuality as sin. "Jesus didn't come to condemn," says the ministry, reminding seekers of God's love and forgiveness.

Founder Robbi Kenney says, "Now and then God brings healing miraculously. But most often it's a step-by-step process, requiring time and discipline." A young man named Ed described it in this way: "The path that I walked after salvation is one that God alone mapped out. Many times I dragged my feet . . . even began to turn back. But Jesus was there, offering hope and encouragement; offering genuine love; offering the full reality of 'new creaturehood.' "

Although he had been a practicing homosexual, he became celibate, giving the Holy Spirit time to work through thought patterns, defenses, and habits. Eventually he reached the point where he fell in love with a girl for the first time in his life: "Like many ex-gays, I never believed I could be physically attracted to a woman. I had assumed that I would one day get married to a woman whom I loved deeply in the Lord, and together we would 'pray through' on the sexual part of our relationship. . . . As I see God's ideal for love and marriage, I find myself looking forward to the time when I will marry. Surely, love and sex — as the Designer planned them — are among life's most beautiful blessings." [1]

Wholeness

We may need to be healed of the wounds caused by living in sin. One woman often prays with those who feel deeply sorry for having an abortion and ask the Lord's forgiveness. She said, "Jesus shows he is there. He loves the girl without condemnation. He indicates he loves her even though she rejected his gift. Often he gives the girl the sense that he is taking the child to be with him and will care for it until she comes to be with him."

---

1. Robbi Kenney, "Once Gay, Always Gay?" *Christian Life,* September 1978, p. 22.

Often the Spirit deals with such wounds in a gradual way, taking one area after another to bring healing over a period of months or years. During this time it's especially important to have the support and fellowship of other believers, solid teaching, personal devotions, reliable Christian counseling, and the strengthening of Holy Communion.

In other instances, the Lord intervenes miraculously. Mary, who had been deeply involved in sin before becoming a Christian, told about attending a workshop on spiritual and emotional wholeness. "I came there as a Christian," she said. "I knew without doubt I had been forgiven. But that afternoon God's love flowed over me. In one moment he healed every one of the wounds left by ten years of sin."

To each of us comes a daily challenge: Do we live in the tornado of sin? But to each comes the ongoing possibility—God's storm shelter: forgiveness through the death and resurrection of Jesus Christ.

And with the forgiveness, joy, because we are set free! After the shelter comes the rainbow.

7
*False guilt occurs when we listen
to the accusations of Satan,
then begin to accuse ourselves.*

How to Leave Guilt Behind

Jack is a workaholic. Fran jumps from one project to another, continually striving, always making excessive demands on those around her. Both Sally and Greg are restless—seldom feeling satisfied with anything, whether home, work, or pleasure. Even success ends as a broken dream.

Then there's Sarah. Long ago she asked forgiveness, but still she broods, remembering past sin, never sensing she is free.

Unknown to each other, these individuals share a common problem—seeking the approval of others without having resolved deep-seated feelings of guilt. Like them, most of us struggle with guilt feelings, many of which come to us for real reasons. But we also suffer from another kind of guilt—a false type.

The first thing we need to do is distinguish between true and false guilt. If our situation involces true guilt and the Holy Spirit convicts us, we realize that our thoughts, attitudes, or actions have offended a righteous God. The Spirit shows us the specific sin and what we should do about it: repent. Uncomfortable as it is to admit guilt, there's a relief about the transaction. We understand that God condemns our sin, but loves us as persons.

Yet for every blessing of God—with the exception of peace—Satan offers an imitation. He does not want to show us real sin, and therefore becomes the source of false guilt, replacing the convicting work of the Holy Spirit with condemnation.

Two things may happen. Satan badgers us with problems so numerous we cannot begin to deal with them. Or, if we ask forgiveness, we do not come to the peace that follows the conviction and repentance brought by the Holy Spirit.

Satan's name means "accuser," and John described him as "the accuser of our brothers" (Rev. 12:10). False guilt occurs when we listen to his accusations, whether they come through the conversation and suggestions of others, or through our ability to accuse ourselves. In contrast to the Spirit's work from deep within, false guilt comes from sources outside us. When we internalize those thoughts, we begin slogging in mud. We will never feel comfortable with someone who falsely accuses us.

To sum it up, we can *be* guilty and *feel* guilty, but if we confess our sin, God removes both the guilt and the feeling of guilt. By contrast, Satan makes us *feel* guilty, even if we aren't.

If we listen to the Holy Spirit, dealing with the sin he calls to our attention, God quietly and decisively forgives. The longer we refuse his work, however, the more uncomfortable his spotlight becomes.

By contrast, what happens under Satan's spotlight? His accusations make any problem seem overwhelming. In bringing condemnation upon us, he cleverly robs us of the joy of our salvation.

The difference between true guilt and false guilt can be seen in this way:

True guilt	False guilt
The Holy Spirit ↓ brings conviction based on truth	Satan ↓ brings condemnation based on lies
His objective: my improvement	*His objective:* my defeat
He spotlights: specific unforgiven sin	*He spotlights:* me in past, forgiven sin, failure of "all those things"
My reaction: "Yes, I have done something wrong." I'm remorseful and repent: "Lord, I'm sorry. Please forgive me."	*My reaction:* helplessness, feeling of a no-win situation. Don't know where to start making a change. If I ask forgiveness, no peace.
God's action: grace, forgiveness, love	*Satan's action:* accusation
Result in me: peace, sense of being set free, knowledge that I am loved, joy!	*Result in me:* continuing lack of peace, defeat, hopelessness, sense of worthlessness, despair. Often feel physically tired, emotionally and spiritually worn down.

Let's consider some areas in which both true and false guilt occur:

Forgiven sin

"My husband and I had to get married," she said. "For 20 years I've asked Jesus to forgive me, but I still don't *feel* forgiven."

Out of pastoral concern, Vander Warner speaks to this problem: "If we don't get rid of our past, our past will get us." When we enter into a sin, Satan knows we're vulnerable for a lifetime of harassment. If your confession of sin doesn't seem real to you, go into a room by yourself. Speaking aloud, tell Jesus you're sorry. Ask his forgiveness. Memorize and repeat the words of 1 John 1:9: To those who repent comes the promise, "If we confess our sins, he is faithful and just and will forgive us our sins and *purify* us from *all* unrighteousness."

In the innermost part of your spirit, you know if you have confessed a sin and determined, by the power of the Holy Spirit, to turn from it. Don't judge forgiveness by your feelings. You will never feel that you are good enough. *You have to take God at his word. The Lord always offers forgiveness, but you need to receive that forgiveness.*

When Satan returns to remind you of a sin you have already confessed, don't argue with him. You will lose. Immediately repeat God's promise: "I will not remember their sins and their wrongs any more" (Heb. 10:17 Beck). If God doesn't remember your forgiven sins, why should you?

The "if onlys"

"I failed," said a father, speaking about his rebellious daughter. "It's hopeless. I just plain failed. If only. . . ."

Miles away, a mother echoed his feeling as she referred to her own situation: "If only I had done things differently when my son was young, he would be a better person now."

The death of a loved one may open the door to similar feelings: "If only I had spent more time with my husband before he died. If only we had taken that trip we talked about."

What about those areas in which we did our best at the time, but now look back and feel guilty? If you're unsure about whether you were right or wrong, you always have the option of going before the Lord and asking forgiveness. If the individual is still alive, you can seek out the person you believe you wronged.

But if the situation about which you grieve involves someone who died, ask the Lord to comfort you with the deep down assurance that your loved one no longer needs a long trip, or whatever you feel you should have done. True, *you* would enjoy that memory, but if your loved one died in the Lord, he or she has something much better.

Once you have taken care of the Spirit-prompted solutions, guard against Satan's condemnation, especially if you don't see an immediate change in your situation. When we tell ourselves, "If only, if only . . ." we think in circles. Circular thinking is fruitless. There comes a point where we spend so much time looking inward that we forget to look upward. Sometimes the very best remedy can be taking a long daily walk in fresh air or pursuing some other form of exercise.

Then return home and do battle. Once you have asked forgiveness for failures of the past, whether real or imagined, God takes care of them. Paul wrote: "So there is now no condemnation awaiting those who belong to Christ Jesus. For the power of the life-giving Spirit — and this power is mine through Christ Jesus — has freed me from the vicious circle of sin and death" (Rom. 8:1-2 LB).

Out of my struggle with the "if onlys" I learned a prayer: "Lord, use even my mistakes for your good." God puts it this way: " 'Forget the former things; do not dwell on the past. See, I am doing a new thing! Now it springs up; do you not perceive it? I am making a way in the desert and streams in the wasteland' " (Isa. 43:18-19).

Self-imposed "I shoulds"

"In general, guilt comes from people having a mind-set about should," said my friend Jane. "We should do this or that. We carry our shoulds from childhood to adulthood and don't always evaluate them."

She gave the example of an exhausted father who comes home from work saying, "I should go to all my son's activities. If I don't, I feel guilty." Or a mother thinks, "I should spend more time with my children." Together a husband and wife may say, "We should be more involved in community organizations." Or, "We should lead a Bible class."

"Then," says Jane, "we come to some questions: What is a

68

true should and what is a false one? What is true guilt because we *should* be spending more time with our children, or teaching at church, or working in the community? And what is a false guilt, because we are already doing our best in priority places?"

We must never throw away all the shoulds. They're what keep us from robbing a bank or going through a stoplight. God also uses the shoulds in our life to convict and bring us to his righteousness. But in some cases only a person who is honest before God knows whether an "I should" is an honest one — something to which God calls. The areas in which we need to be particularly careful appear when we ask, "Is my 'I should' a matter of misplaced priorities or pride?" Am I thinking, *I can control my situation, even my health; I can do everything perfectly, no matter how much I take on?*

If our expectations of self are too low, the Holy Spirit will convict us. If they are too high, we may be suffering under the false guilt and condemnation of Satan that makes us feel we must be all things to all people. If we feel pushed in every direction, even by valuable "I shoulds," a reliance on God can be our best defense against condemnation.

The busier I am, the more I need time alone with God each morning. From those moments I take at least one thought with me. In an amazing way, I find that it gives direction to my day. Out of his peace, I begin thinking, "A, B, or C priority." By making my top priority time with God, I discover that some things I thought were important really aren't. Other things that I would have sidestepped turn out to be vital, and I sense his blessing on them.

Expectations of others

"If you love me, prove it," says the boy in the backseat of a car, urging a girl to fit his standards (which, of course, are nonexistent). If she feels guilty about saying no, she can easily fall into sin.

A difficulty in saying no can also trigger false guilt in any of us because of our need for the approval of others. Take the problem of too many requests for our time. We feel guilty because we cannot stretch far enough, and guilty if we say no. To compound the problem, if we enjoy a measure of success in an area of service, we see one opportunity after another open up. Many will be of God. Some might be distractions. We'll know the difference when we become so busy that even the work we normally do well shows mediocrity.

The expectations of others can work for our betterment or detriment. We decide which it will be. Jesus said, "No one who puts his hand to the plow and looks back is fit for service in the kingdom of God" (Luke 9:62). When torn in every direction, we in effect look back, no longer seeing where we are going. We become unfit for service.

If we are exhausted and guilt-ridden, we may be trying to be persons God never called us to be. Pastor and author Bob Mumford writes of a parable in which a duck, rabbit, squirrel, and eagle were all forced to take the same curriculum of running, swimming, climbing, and flying. As a result, they received injuries or suffered overexertion which reduced all of them to the same level. No one did anything well.

Mumford offers five symptoms to help us recognize when we may be overextending ourselves, entering areas for which God has not equipped us: competition, a growing sense of inadequacy, defensiveness, despair, and breakdown.[1]

If we feel overextended, we need to recognize the specific circle of influence in which God desires to use us. Often I ask myself, "What is the one thing I can do that no one else can do?" It helps me weed out the unnecessary and reminds me of my commitment to live in the center of God's will, not veering to the right or to the left.

When we know that will, we don't have the right to be more obedient to the requests of others than to God. As Jane put it, "When I do what someone else expects me to do, rather than

---

1. Bob Mumford, "Back Over the Barbwire!" *New Wine* (January, 1983, pp. 4, 6). The parable is from *Inside the Ark Learning Center* and "What's Going On Here," Springfield, Oregon, Public Schools Newsletter, Vol. 1, No. 8, February 8, 1975.

what I know is right in God's sight, I am being untrue to my own values."

This "head knowledge" works down into practical areas when we ask God to reveal to us the gift or combination of gifts in which God has motivated us to serve (see Rom. 12:4-8). We also learn to be unflinching about those things to which God tells us to say no. Time-management expert Dennis Hensley gives this guideline in *Staying Ahead of Time:* "Before you say 'yes' to a future commitment, check to see if you have time for it *now*. If you don't, you won't have time later. Say 'no' " (p. 36).

In *The Light and the Glory,* Peter Marshall and David Manuel issue a challenge that is not an excuse for doing nothing, but a release from being troubled about many things: "God does not take the measure of men's lives by the sum of their accomplishments. Rather, in the case of the founding of America, He seems to have been more concerned with the quality and depth of commitment" (p. 79).

In the book of Revelation John looks forward to the day when Satan meets ultimate defeat: "For the accuser of our brothers, who accuses them before our God day and night, has been hurled down. They overcame him by the blood of the Lamb and by the word of their testimony; they did not love their lives so much as to shrink from death" (12:10-11).

The accusations of Satan can be compared to a winter wind—shrieking around the corner, tearing away at our peace, difficult to face, and always bringing misery. To continue walking in the bitter cold, we must turn our back to the wind, casting down the accuser, as we refuse to keep company with him.

By contrast, the Holy Spirit moves as a gentle wind on a day when spring comes quietly. As we welcome him into every part of our being, he brings the cleansing of soft rain, breathes in new life and joy, and leaves a sense of the faithfulness of God. The daffodils and tulips left dormant by the cold of winter burst from the ground and bloom.

So begins a flowering in our life.

8 *When we choose to be faithful,*
God undergirds our choice
with his faithfulness.

Windproof Your Marriage

In a July 3rd storm straight-line winds in excess of 100 miles an hour ripped off a portion of our roof, hurled it against the chimney, causing it to crack, stripped wiring, snapped plumbing, and uprooted numerous large, treasured trees. Water poured in, and that night mice found a new home within ours.

To every person who commiserated with us my husband and I said, "We'll make it. We'll have it back in shape in no time." We stepped around the branches in our bedroom, sloshed through the puddles filling half the house, and told ourselves, "We'll dig in and be all right."

After three days of this, I woke up feeling tied in knots. When I exploded at something inconsequential, my husband said quietly, "Loie, why don't we just stop telling ourselves everything is okay? Why don't we admit we're really upset about all the damage? Then let's go on from there."

For the first time since the storm I laughed honestly, not just in an attempt to be courageous. He had expressed the problem perfectly. We hugged each other and went back to carrying our belongings outside to dry.

There is no home without at least occasional times of tension, if not frequent ones. Whatever the cause—storm damage, work layoff, inadequate financial resources, loneliness, serious illness, children gone wrong—there's one result. When our difficulties pile up, they play havoc with our relationships. Hard times either widen the gap or bring us closer together.

When we experience such times, what thoughts might help us as husband and wife to pull together, even grow in our love? How can we persevere?

Commit yourself

We begin marriage with high hopes, but at one time or another most people question the rightness of their commitment. When crises occur or daily routine makes life seem ho-hum, it's easy to think, "The honeymoon is over; what do I do now? If only I had married someone else, everything would be perfect. Was it *really* God's will that I married this person?"

To the last question we can immediately respond, *If you are married, it has become God's will, even if it wasn't before.* Stick with your marriage. Such questions really ask one thing: "Would I be happier with a different partner?"

My friend Judy was divorced in spite of doing everything she could to keep her marriage together. She talked about the problem of married people believing they would be better off elsewhere: "They think, 'I'm so unhappy I want to get out of it.' I want to tell them, 'You don't know what unhappiness is until you've been through a divorce.'"

She referred to a friend's problem: "She has a man out there who's available. It's tempting her. She thinks she can walk out of her marriage and have him. There's no guarantee it will work out right." Judy's comment acknowledges that in addition to the sin involved, most people bring the same problems to a second marriage.

Contrary to popular belief, love isn't something that just happens. All of us choose to love or not love. Every person still married has decided individually and as part of a couple to continue loving, even when the honeymoon ended. We don't always recognize it under those terms, but that's what actually happens.

We make such choices with our will. If you and I enter marriage feeling it is a throwaway commodity, it *will* become disposable. When difficult days come and we think there's an option for something easier, we stop working on what we have at home.

In the course of marriage many couples meet temptation. But what if we make a once-for-all commitment to faithfulness and tell ourselves, "I will not even entertain the idea of leaving this marriage"? When we determine that breaking our marital vow is not an option, we face temptation and adversity from a stronger point.

One person said, "I refuse to think about betraying my mate, even if it seems innocent fooling around." That choice includes a refusal to fantasize about what could be, or might-have-been. As marriage counselor J. Allan Peterson explains in *The Myth of the Greener Grass,* "Fantasies are a preview to the desired action. An affair is experienced many times in fantasy before the time and place of the first rendezvous is set" (p. 87).

A couple summarized their feelings about commitment: "We work at our marriage, using differences of opinion as an opportunity to grow. We try to recognize and immediately say no to requests that ask something we should not give. No matter what happens we are committed to one another before God and man. Through the power of the Holy Spirit we renew that commitment every day by saying, 'I love you.' "

God is on the side of a marriage staying together. When partners choose to be faithful for better or for worse, he supports their choice: "To the faithful you show yourself faithful" (Ps. 18:25).

Communicate

"We had been married at least five years," said Karen, "when suddenly my husband asked, 'Why do you always fry the bacon so hard?' I myself don't like crisp bacon, but for years I made it that way, thinking I was pleasing him." She recognized it as a symptom of a deeper need to communicate. When a variety of difficult situations confronted them, they learned to work at that communication.

Their situation is not untypical. Ideally we should develop communication skills *before* difficult times. If, instead, you are already facing adversity, ask the Holy Spirit to help you learn constructive ways to deal with what is happening to you.

"Before marriage all of us talk about love and plans for the future, and we think that's communication," said Cheryl. "But it goes much deeper than 'I'm going to be home at five,' or, 'I'll take the kids there.' That's surface communication."

Communication at the level we need grows from a combination of things that are right, one of these being a commitment to spend time together on a regular basis. If we face a number of problems, it becomes even more difficult to find quality time together. Yet without communication, problems multiply. One professional person writes a date with his wife into the calendar. Nothing interferes except an emergency.

Such times should involve more than side-by-side togetherness, although nonverbal moments are also needed. It's crucial to have enough breathing space that even a hesitant talker can begin. In *The Intimate Marriage* Howard and Charlotte Clinebell offer several recommendations for better communication, among them the following:

• Check out meanings by asking questions such as, "Do I hear you correctly?" Or "Is this what you are saying?"

• Learn the skill of saying something straight: "Each person can help the other to understand by asking himself, 'Am I saying what I really mean?' "

• Learn to translate coded and contradictory messages. Without being aware of what we are doing, we may say one thing and live another because we have not resolved inner conflicts. These need to be brought out in the open and discussed.

I would like to add other ideas I've gleaned:

• Unbox your loved ones. One woman consistently says, "My son is so quiet. He never talks." Another wife reports the same problem with her husband.

It's easy to put a person into a box and tell them by our words or actions to stay there. We were guests in a home where the host asked our 13-year-old son a question. Without thinking, I answered for him. My husband did me a great, long-term favor when he said, "Loie, I believe he wanted Jeff to answer."

• Keep mind reading in perspective. Rebecca complained about her unmet needs. When asked, "Does your husband know you feel this way?" she replied, "No. I just feel he should know me well enough to *know*."

Phil expressed a similar problem, and felt afraid to tell his wife, "I'm discouraged. Build me up. Make me feel I'm worth something." As husband or wife, all of us should be willing to express needs, listen, and respond to the heart cries of the other. When we grow together, we learn to sense those cries, even without words. Yet our sensing should not be a substitute for that which needs to be communicated, simply by saying, "Tell me more."

• Go beyond "I think" to "I feel." Cheryl put it this way: "Feelings are neither right or wrong. For years I didn't realize that, and if my husband and I disagreed, I took it personally. I thought he didn't want to do anything with me. So many people are hurt and don't let out their feelings. They're afraid of another person's judgment."

Feelings come unbidden, and it's what we do about them that becomes right or wrong. I asked Cheryl how she began communicating her needs. "I started saying, 'I feel,' and then finished it," she said. "Then I hoped the other person wouldn't take personally my efforts to communicate problems. I used to lambast my husband when he came in the door, saying, 'Where have you been?' He thought I was complaining. I learned to tell him, 'I'm lonely,' or 'I'm angry.' A counselor gave me a list of the feeling words. I didn't have them in my vocabulary. I had to identify what my feelings were, then begin to express them."

• Forget about winning. It didn't seem to matter to Jesus whether he won his arguments with the Pharisees. Outwardly he seemed to lose in going to the cross, but it became his ultimate gift.

Within the marriage bond there is no such thing as a win/lose situation. A secure person does not have to be right in every situation. Those who continually win arguments usually lose the marriage. As Jesus said, a "household divided against itself will not stand" (Matt. 12:25).

After celebrating their 27th anniversary, one couple still remembers something my father said during their wedding service: "Before you go to bed at night, either agree, or agree to disagree. That way you'll always be in agreement."

This kind of agreement does not rule out having opinions of your own. It means, instead, that you have learned to deal with them. A neighbor asked Beverly, a widow about to be remarried, "How can you stand to have those trees in your backyard cut down? You've guarded them with your life, and now your fiancé wants to build a garage there." Beverly shrugged and smiled: "You give a little, you receive a little."

• Let others support you. During a year when our lives were buffeted by many forms of wind, three other couples felt led by God to encourage my husband and me through a support group. The eight of us met in one another's homes, studied Scripture together, sang, and prayed. Any confidences we shared stayed within the group. By the end of the year we had developed a level of trust where our party facades were put away and honest, deep-level sharing surfaced even in hurried telephone conversations. Though we no longer meet regularly, we still enjoy a high priority commitment to one another.

Face reality

If strong winds and torrential rain assail our home, we shut the windows. It's the realistic thing to do. When difficult times enter our lives, we may need to be just as realistic.

Healthy communication should lay the groundwork for the ability to make decisions together. When things go wrong it's easy for one to say, "You got me into this." The other replies, "You wanted something, and I let you have it, even though it wasn't my choice."

If we are to pull together in every circumstance, there are four words we need to set aside: *It's all your fault.* If you feel your present problems really are the result of one of you overwhelming the other in a past decision, ask forgiveness. Bury it. Refuse to bring it up again. Go on from that point.

Forgiveness is not just something we give, but a whole way of life, even a refusal to utter two deadly sentences: "I told you so," and "If only you had listened to me." Forgiveness means leaving the past behind—even the guilt or resentment we feel regarding it. If we truly forgive, we restore dignity by loving our partner without reservation, and without acting as though we expect the same problem again.

My husband nailed a two-by-six across two widely spaced stumps and carried it to the top of a high hill. He knows I like to sit there, that often I need the long view—across a field and pond, and up a steep, wooded bank to the distant horizon. More than that, he was quietly telling me something else. I can't recall the reason for my angry words of the night before, but I remember his postscript—his way of saying, "I'm not perfect, and you're not perfect, but I love you."

When we face difficult times, our children can be supportive, or they can recognize their advantage. Facing reality means refusing to allow them to drive a wedge between us as husband and wife, so that we take sides against each other. By contrast, however, facing reality can also mean letting your loved ones see you cry.

When we are upset, afraid, or tense, it's easy to forget the feelings of children. Though we hide our emotions, they sense them. Often the unknown is more frightening than the real thing. We won't be of use to anyone if we become maudlin about a situation, but there's a difference between that and letting others know we hurt.

One of the most wounded people I have ever known comes from a home in which her parents never showed anything but strength. If we do the same, even in the very worst circumstances, we threaten everyone around us. There's a time when we have to be strong in order to encourage others. There's another time when we say, "I'm scared too. I'm also hurting. I don't know what's going to happen." To do otherwise puts too great a burden on the person who feels inadequate. Then, after being honest about our needs, we can work together to find the promises of God, asking for all the power of the Holy Spirit.

Working together also means making time for sex. If you sense your world is falling apart there may be 100 reasons why you don't take the time needed for intimacy. Your bedroom can be a haven against the cares of the world. Don't make sex a performance. Think about the pleasure of your partner and how you can help your husband or wife relax.

If the hard times you've shared have raised invisible barriers between you, you might want to offer two prayers: "Help me deal with any conflict hindering our intimacy," and "Give me a greater love for my marriage partner than ever before." Expect to receive that love. You will.

Keep on keeping on

Too much pressure and an inability to express needs can bring any one of us to a breaking point. When times are difficult our problems multiply. One bad situation sometimes becomes the catalyst for another. If you wonder whether life is worth living anymore, if you find yourself being violent or the object of an abusive situation, ask for help.

When William Barclay comments on Paul's statement that love is patient, he says the Greek word that is used always describes patience with people, not patience with circumstances. In many marriages there comes a need to work out a strategy for dealing with serious problems such as abuse, alcoholism, or ongoing unfaithfulness. If this occurs, and you are the injured person, go to a respected Christian counselor who will encourage your wish to keep your marriage together. Such a person won't be shocked by your difficulties. He or she will bring the grace of God to your situation, offering positive steps of correction.

In time of hardship Cam and Maxine Hancock have often prayed that the Lord would never let both of them go down together. Carol Sherry came to the same passage in Ecclesiastes when she sought the Lord about whether to marry Jim: "Though one may be overpowered, two can defend themselves," wrote Solomon. "A cord of three strands is not quickly broken" (Eccles. 4:12).

"I realized that if there's two people, there's really three," said Carol. "If there's only one, there's really two. We're never alone. There's always that extra person, just as for Shadrach, Meschach, and Abednego. When they walked in the fiery furnace, there was a fourth person with them."

When we keep Jesus Christ as the third person in our marriage, we begin to see our home as a place of refuge in spite of 100-mile-an-hour winds. Think again of his gift to us. When we choose to be faithful, he undergirds our choice with his faithfulness.

An elm stood on our property for many years before being cut down. From the outside, the tree appeared to be one. At a horizontal cut a third of the way up, it *was* one. But near the earth a cross section revealed two separate and individual trunks. Over the years they had grown so completely together that even the bark surrounded and covered them.

All of us enter a marital relationship as two separate and unique individuals. Whenever we hold out, afraid of losing our individuality or privileges, we remain divided. If, instead, we give ourselves one to the other, willing to keep on keeping on, we grow more and more together. We gain a strength we would never have alone. We stand united against the winds of difficulty.

Love grows over the cracks that would divide us.

9

*Have you reached the end
of your emotional capacity?
Because of God's faithfulness,
you can enter a process:*

Learn to Love Unconditionally

Her dark brown hair was drawn back, yet here and there a tendril escaped, wisping softly around her face. In a quiet, yet confident voice she spoke, with only her eyes, and occasionally her tightly clenched hands, betraying her pain.

"It's a process," she said. "A long process. It has taken years for me to reach the point where I can even talk about it. When I look back, I see how far I've come. Some time from now, it will probably surprise me how far beyond this point I've moved."

I will call her Erica, and her husband John. Theirs is the story of an 11-year anguish over their daughter's behavior. Out of their deep love for Pam, they suffer still, and the situation is unresolved. I asked Erica what she has learned that would help other parents with their children:

"People come to us, knowing Pam has been in deep trouble," she said. "They think perhaps their child is starting to use drugs, and they are desperate. I tell them, 'Deal with it right away. Confront them now, and keep confronting them in love.

John and I both admit we did the wrong thing. We thought, *We're going to ride it out. It's going to get better.* That's why it's necessary to be open and confronting. Confrontation comes from a heart of love, not a heart of condemnation. Do all that you can to help in constructive ways, but allow them to take responsibility for their own wrong behavior."

She continued: "It's hardest, probably, to forgive myself for my lack of awareness of what was happening. It was as though I stuck my head in the sand, not wanting to know. I thought it was merely a state of rebellion—a normal independence for kids that age, because I didn't understand the symptoms of deviant behavior.

"Pam went to counseling once and wouldn't return. When we tried to go as a family, she refused. She agreed to go by herself, but came home saying, 'They were busy. I couldn't get in.' Already she was covering, and we didn't realize it, because there was no evidence around the house. We should have recognized her behavior. But it could *never* happen to our daughter! We now think she was using cocaine before she left home at 18. At some point after that she entered the prostitution that is often a part of drug abuse."

Erica spoke of the need for communication: "Pam has always found it difficult to talk about feelings. When a situation got a little tight, or there was a lot of talking going on, she removed herself from it. Over and over she's been running.

"Parents should help their children express how they feel. Ask questions, and allow thoughts and emotions to come out without expressing judgment about them. Bottled-up emotions can become explosive later on.

"We kept the communication going at all costs. Back when I knew she was having problems, but before I understood fully what she was into, I started calling her once a week. At that time she repeatedly said, 'I'm busy. I'll call you back.' I still felt she needed that call. So I kept it up, or dropped a card in the mail to let her know I loved her. I had the need to do that. It was also a burden, because I wondered, *Am I alienating her more?* I did this for seven years whenever I knew where she lived. It helped me to hear her voice and know she was still alive.

"I tried to convey love without smothering her. At times we *couldn't* communicate. We didn't have an address, or a way to call her. When you don't hear from someone for months, you don't know where they are, or even *if* they are.

"Up to then, I never knew what it meant to cry out to the Lord. Now I know that when we get to that point, God supplies something, such as a telephone call. After not hearing from Pam for six months, I prayed, 'Lord, I don't know how I'm going to get through the day without knowing where she is.' Within a week Pam called."

Ruefully she smiled. "We came back into contact because she wrote two bad checks, apparently to buy cocaine. My husband could have prosecuted her, but we used it as an opportunity to get her into the counseling she refused for years."

Feelings of guilt and rejection can be a real problem in this kind of situation. Erica talked about dealing with both: "In a counseling session Pam expressed a desire to 'do more things with mom—things like lunch and shopping.' In the delusion of drug abuse individuals say what they think the counselor or parents would like to hear. It's not necessarily what they themselves think. Maybe in one sense Pam *does* want more contact with me, but in another sense she can't handle it. Her love affair with the drug is too great. Then, too, those on chemicals are used to manipulation for survival. They say things they think will pacify whoever it is so they can continue hanging onto their drug.

"I gave her opportunities to do something together, but nothing came of it. The inability to plan ahead is another symptom of drug abuse. Following the next counseling session, I was able to express to her that if she would like to come out and talk with me, it would make me happy. But it would have to be her initiative. She must contact me, because I could no longer handle the rejection. After several years I had reached the end of my emotional capacity."

I asked Erica what thought she hangs onto when struggling with rejection: "God loves me, no matter how I reject him by not following or doing as he would have me do. I tell him I'm sorry for those wrong things I know I've done. I also realize that I reject him in ways I'm not even aware. Yet he still loves me. I want to love Pam with the same unconditional love. The hurt is so deep that it doesn't come easily. *It's a process* involving a lot of anguish, not a quick fix.

"Any guilt is difficult. Real guilt was easier for me to deal with, because I was able to confess it and receive peace. I also realized that though I was far from perfect, as I had tried to be, God knew the intent in my heart was to be a good mother. When I first learned Pam was in trouble, I asked myself, 'How could I have gone so wrong when I meant so well?' There was a lot of self-examination, and as I repented about what may have been wrong words or actions, I knew God did forgive me and love me as he always had. The burden lifted.

"Also, it was easier to deal with guilt when I realized all that is involved for persons abusing drugs. There were other factors at work in Pam's life, such as the influence of older girls, wrong peer pressure, a rebellious spirit, and mind altering drugs. Persons such as Pam lose control of themselves, and that becomes a reason for patterns of negative behavior. But often I wanted to take all the guilt on myself, so I could confess and get rid of it.

"False guilt was a real battle. I believe Satan's desire was to absolutely cripple me. The most difficult guilt trip came during the first couple of years when he fed me the lie that no one would value what I said or did anymore, because of the failure I had been. I felt that anything I did for the Lord wouldn't be blessed.

"There were times when I wanted to withdraw into depression and self-pity. Then one day I realized *I had a choice*. I could accept what Satan wanted to do to me. *Or* I could move out with more determination and zeal in whatever way the Lord wanted to use me. Whenever we are in a crisis situation it's important to ask, 'Lord, what do you want me to do in this?'

The turning point came when I shook my fist at Satan and said, 'You're tampering with Pam's life, but you're not going to have mine.' It's important to not allow yourself to lose the sense of God's love for you because that's the basis of respect for yourself."

I wondered if it had been hard for Erica to not be in control of what was happening. "Yes," she answered emphatically. "That's part of the yielding, the relinquishment, the letting go. Society and my own humanness have geared me to figure out solutions for problems that arise in everyday living. Often I forget the supernatural power of God. The enormity of my problem and my repeated failure have caused me to rely totally on God. I've learned to look to the future with more hope and trust, knowing he is in control of the situation.

"In the past I have been overly concerned about whatever I say and do. We were always told, 'Actions speak louder than words.' But I couldn't be a perfect mother. Then, in my desire to give my children a picture of right and wrong actions, I pointed out things that were wrong. Pam picked it out as judgment. I didn't clarify the important difference between correct behavior and love for the person. We accept and love a person, but we do not or must not accept wrong behavior.

"There were times when I could not do anything to change the situation with Pam, but I could do positive things for myself, such as joining in-depth Bible study and meaningful support groups, or taking classes to better deal with the problem."

For most of us the middle of the night offers the greatest temptation for falling apart. Erica said, "I would wake up, filled with all sorts of thoughts. So many things could happen to her. I'd pray, 'Lord, I don't know where she is. You take care of her.' Those were points of giving her over, but I feel I am closest to complete relinquishment now. That, too, has been a process. Most of all, I want to keep Pam from suffering. But I have learned to depend on God and whatever is needed to work out his plan for her life."

She spoke of God's protection in times of widespread newspaper and television coverage: "It's interesting how God has taken us away from home both times some big crisis happened in her life. It was as though he were saying, 'I can handle this job all my myself.' We don't know yet, but we wonder if we will look back and see Pam's arrest and public exposure as a turning point.

"The morning the trial was to begin I was distraught, and didn't know what to read for devotions with my husband. We were a long way from Hosea, but I 'happened' to open the Bible to Chapter 2. The entire chapter was a refreshment along the way, as though God were saying to Pam, 'I will betroth you to me in faithfulness; and you shall know the Lord' " (v. 20 RSV; see the entire chapter).

"At first we were tempted to sell our home and move where nobody knew us. I felt sorry for John on the first morning he left for work after it had all been out in the paper. I thought how awful it must be to walk into his office where he is highly respected. But if there has been anything said that wasn't good, we haven't known about it. People loved us, sending supportive notes and Bible verses, as well as telephoning. As a result we have become freer to love. That's something I usually tell parents. Don't worry about hanging on to your dark, hurtful secrets. Let others know, because they're going to reach out and pray for you. They won't have any way of knowing you hurt unless you tell them. It's not easy to walk into a crowd, realizing everybody knows what went on with your child. But if it weren't for that exposure, I probably wouldn't be helping other parents now."

She spoke of dealing with negative feelings by repeating memorized Scripture and hymns, and reading faith-building books and articles. "During a night when I desperately needed comfort, I remembered the second verse of "A Mighty Fortress Is Our God": 'For us the one true Man must fight, the Man of God's own choosing. . . .'

"Through all of this, I have learned to pray for enemies, such as the man who led my daughter into crime. I also recognize that negative attitudes are of Satan and positive, faith thoughts are of God. When I realized that all the discouragement I felt during the trial was actually coming from Satan, not God, what a revelation!

"Best of all, I learned the sustaining power of God's grace. As God said to Paul, 'My grace is sufficient for you, for my power is made perfect in weakness' " (2 Cor. 12:9 RSV).

"My husband went to the trial, and Pam asked him to leave. He told her, 'I'm not going to stay around all the time, Pam, but I want you to know that I won't ever give up on you.'

"Recently he said, 'I've learned not to blame myself anymore for what happened. I'm able to keep my mind on matters at hand better than I used to. Maybe we didn't do everything right—in fact, I know we didn't do everything right—but I also realize that the decision to do wrong was not our decision. Pam did have a choice. Whatever brought her to that choice, we don't know.' "

As Erica thought back over the years, she said, "There were times when the hurt was so deep that I withheld love. I know that the love never left, but my feelings weren't there—the warm feelings I had toward her." She returned to the point of having both love and feelings of love by asking God for help.

"When I see her for just a short time, I am able to give her love. That's God's grace. Even on the day I talked to her about feeling rejected, I was able to put my hand on her arm and say, 'I love you, Pam.' That's one of the many blessings from all this. I have learned the meaning of unconditional love. Christ is now my companion, instead of someone I just reach out to once in awhile.

"I've also learned to pray more specifically for both family and friends. I don't ask just for the comforts of life, but for things that will encourage their spiritual growth. My life is more of a constant praying."

She talked about her expectations for Pam. "Before she got into trouble, I had hopes and dreams of all that I would like to see her do—get married, have a happy family, be happy in the Lord.

"Now I know—and it took awhile—that my expectations cannot be too high, for my own protection. My expectations cannot be there until she gets help in her addiction and God begins to heal her. Holidays are difficult. I have Christmas gifts for the past two years in the closet, because she hasn't shown up to receive them.

"As for the future, I will never give up hope, no matter what happens. I know what I'm seeing now is an acting-out behavior tied in with the drugs and her peer group. Underneath is something beautiful that is going to surface. I believe God is going to use what she has gone through, and it's going to propel her at a greater speed and with more dedication to be the kind of person he wants her to be. It's the verse, 'I will restore to you the years which the swarming locust has eaten' (Joel 2:25 RSV).

"I hang onto the belief that all the prayers haven't been said in vain. I have learned to keep up hope in every situation, and to keep my eyes on the cross. No matter how terrible life gets, we still have that promise. Praise God, he *has* given the victory!

"I visualize Pam as released and radiant. Released from bondage, knowing complete forgiveness from God for her past. Radiant because she is a powerful child of God.

"That hope doesn't come overnight."

In addition to the promises already mentioned, Erica has found these passages especially meaningful: Ps. 108:12-13; Prov. 3:5-6; Isa. 41:10-13; 59:21; Jer. 31:15-17; Hab. 2:3; Rom. 15:13 and 2 Cor. 10:3-6.

10 *Forgiveness should not be mistaken for passivity. Whenever we forgive we receive a blood transfusion.*

God's Remedy for Pain

The angry words were out. A moment later Diane bit her lip, wishing she could swallow every syllable. *I didn't really mean them,* she thought. *I'm under pressure at work, and I take it out on everyone around me. How can I set things straight?*

Recognize the feeling? Maybe you're hurt or frustrated, angry or defeated. You spoke without thinking, or someone spoke too quickly to you. Or you've lost your job, and feel you can't win—even in personal relationships. Now you have a cold ache inside because once more you've said too much, or wanted to say more than you could.

All of us have a basic need to be loved and respected. Yet when love or respect involves either a close or a long-standing relationship, that relationship needs maintenance—the gift of forgiveness. What's more, it is only forgiveness that brings healing after a relationship has been broken. If we sense we are falling apart, needing to experience God's faithfulness, how can we receive his remedy for pain?

Recognize the opportunity

At 18 years of age, Sandra married a person she believed to be a nice, churchgoing boy. Soon after, she learned her husband had spent several years in a federal penitentiary for manslaughter, and had been released as incorrigible. Eventually he was diagnosed as a sociopathic personality.

Sandra and her children experienced his problems in the form of violence and abuse. Never was there enough money for basic necessities. In spite of his marital infidelities and frequent abandonments, she stayed with him. When she was pregnant with their third child, Gary left for the last time.

Early in her marriage Sandra became a Christian, and discovered something essential to every one of us—the *necessity,* yet also the *opportunity,* of being a forgiver. "Unforgiveness is one of the chief reasons for suffering in the first place," she said. "It's a sure way to thwart the flow of God's grace in your life. It also defeats your capacity to cope. The energy force of a grudge tends to drive evil toward you."

Because of the abusive situation in which Sandra lived, she had to do some spiritual housecleaning—forgiving every person and circumstance that had hurt her. She explained: "I made a list of all the real and imagined offenses committed against me. Then I burned it. When the list went up in flames and became ashes, it could not be brought back together in its original form. In the same way, as I forgave, the offenses against me were gone. They didn't exist anymore."

Remove the chains

Forgiveness is the best way to extinguish the anger that burns inside us. Yet there is never a "good" time to forgive. It needs to be accomplished immediately, before the knife turns and produces an even larger wound.

That's where Jesus doesn't let us down. Through his anguish and death on the cross, he provided for our forgiveness. By praying, "Father, forgive them," he showed us how to forgive others.

In John 20:23 Jesus told his disciples, "If you forgive the

sins of any, they are forgiven; if you retain the sins of any, they are retained" (RSV). If we are to be disciples to a dying world, we have no choice but to forgive those who have hurt us. When we delay, we retain their sins in the form of negative feelings. Our anger turns inward, and we grow increasingly resentful, bitter, and depressed.

Jody knew she should forgive and began praying, "Lord, I *want* to forgive. . . ." I stopped her: "Jody, just forgive. Right now." Together we prayed the John 20:23 prayer: "Jesus, in your name I forgive the person who hurt me. I ask you to bless that person. Forgive me for any resentment or bitterness I feel."

With those words Jody asked God to remove the chains around the young man who had hurt her. Her prayer did not necessarily remove *every* chain, because he may have hurt others also. But in effect Jody prayed, "Lord, I don't want the way he wronged me to hinder your work in his life. Take off the chains, Lord. Reach him in those ways he needs you."

In a variety of situations people tell me, "I can't forgive." Or, "I can forgive, but I can't ask the Lord to bless that person." Both forgiveness and blessing are given or withheld through a decision. Because you and I have free will, we choose to forgive, or to continue living in anger and resentment. The first time we offer the John 20:23 prayer after being deeply hurt, our emotions will probably not be in it. Good feelings may not come until the 20th prayer. *Yet God hears the first time, because we pray with our will, according to his command.* At the right time he gives us the needed feelings.

Following this prayer Bob said, "I never knew *how* to forgive my wife and her boyfriend. In the moment I prayed, God took all the hurt, the anger, and the bitterness from me. I feel like a different person!"

After years of buried hurt and a long stint on chemotherapy, one woman prayed about the husband from whom she had been divorced early in life. As she finished, tears of relief coursed down her cheeks. "I knew I had to take care of it!" she exclaimed. "I knew I had to forgive! But I didn't know how, because he died long ago." Subsequently her good health was confirmed by doctors.

Once we have forgiven, it's important to ask God to restore wholeness. To make it real I visualize the person who hurt me, as well as the surroundings where it happened. Then I ask Jesus to come into the room. I think of his love for both of us and pray, "Jesus, bring your healing." When I am honest in asking, the Lord is faithful in answering. He doesn't waste pain.

Talk about it

Often such a prayer releases the healing we desperately need. Other times we don't become whole persons until we begin communicating. With many of us that's a problem, for when we truly hurt we stop talking. One husband recognized his wife's anguish over a professional insult when he said, "I've never known my wife to be so upset. She absolutely could not speak. She couldn't even tell me what happened."

When someone hurts or mistreats us, we often think, "I don't dare tell my husband (or my wife, my best friend, or my pastor) how I feel. He might think even worse of me, and I can't handle any more failure." Refusing to talk about hurt or anger has the same result as failing to forgive—our feelings turn inward. When we deal with anger we take a necessary step in leaving depression behind.

It's important that we express our feelings to a trusted person and then pray the John 20:23 prayer. In some instances God may want us to go a step further—to discuss the situation with the one who hurt us.

Nancy talked about a long-standing grievance at work. "I felt I should go to Wayne, my supervisor, and say, 'I forgive you,' even though he didn't realize there was a need for forgiveness. But I certainly argued with God. I didn't *want* to go. Then I sensed his prompting: 'You do it anyway, even if you don't feel like it.'

"I thought I had forgiven and received healing before, but this time it was as if the healing was complete. Later on, another person was upset with Wayne and came to me, wanting to complain. I told him, 'I'm sorry. Wayne and I have reconciled, and I can't break that reconciliation.'"

Ninety-nine percent of the time when I have made a move toward forgiveness, the other person has shown relief. Yet even if they don't know how to respond by giving forgiveness, I have fulfilled my part by saying and meaning, "I forgive you."

Whenever forgiveness occurs, it's important to restore dignity. Richard Hanson writes, "Real forgiveness requires a resolution of all feelings to the point of equal honor for both parties. Both must see each other as worthy and good. They must part with equal dignity. True forgiveness leaves the offender with as much innocence as the offended."

To give dignity to another, we may need to sacrifice our self-righteousness and our desire to win. As one friend put it, "I don't have to be Mrs. Right on every occasion." She wanted the forgiven person to be her friend, not someone who would always be uncomfortable with her.

Pay the price

The communication required to reach forgiveness can be painful, but God never wastes pain. We may waste time in moving beyond it, but God does not waste pain itself. When you and I talk in a healthy way about things that bother us, we take a step toward wholeness.

Four of us were gathered around the kitchen table—my husband Roy and I, one of our sons, and his steady girl friend. Our son made a comment. Without thinking, I added to the problem. Then Roy did something that indicated how much he's grown through the hard times we have shared. Once he would have remained silent, never telling us we had hurt him. I was proud of him when he quietly remarked, "What you said bothers me. I think we need to talk about it."

We discussed the situation, which was more my fault than anyone's, and our son and I asked forgiveness. But the healing would never have come if Roy hadn't been willing to pay the price of communication.

Most of us are afraid of the other person's reaction to our request for better understanding. Only once have I received an even deeper wound. When I asked forgiveness, the person replied, "Yes, I forgive you. But you also did this, and this, and this." To each wrong, whether real or imagined, I answered, "Will you forgive me for that also?" After half an hour, I could bear no more, and quietly finished the conversation.

As soon as I was alone, the tears came—a torrent of them. When I dried my swollen eyes, I realized something had changed—not in the person, but in me. I had always thought, *It's all my fault. If I keep on trying, I can make the situation right. Our relationship will be perfect.* That day God absolved false guilt and removed my feelings of rejection, giving me the sense, "You have done your best. It's in my hands."

Whose problem?

In a Bible class Penny Stokes deepened my awareness of the domino effect of deception. Jacob deceived his father concerning his birthright, but in seeking Laban's permission to marry Rachel, he began reaping what he had sown. His father-in-law was even more deceptive. Tricked into marrying Leah, Jacob worked 14 years for Rachel, but again used deception—this time to increase his herds. After a harvest of many heartaches, including the lies of his 10 sons about his beloved Joseph's safety, Jacob evaluated his life: "My years have been few and difficult, and they do not equal the years of the pilgrimage of my fathers" (Gen. 47:9).

Meanwhile, what happened to Leah, who desperately needed to be loved? Whose problem was it? Hers or Jacob's? Or Laban's? Yet did she feel everything was all her fault?

When we need to forgive, you and I may come to the place where we have to make an honest evaluation—not to blame others, but to come to peace. We may need to say, "I've done all I can to be a person worthy of love, but I cannot force someone to love me." For the first time, perhaps, we decide, "I cannot change my circumstances, *but through the power of the Holy Spirit* I can change my reaction to them."

In that moment we recognize, not with judgment, but with discernment, "It's not my problem. I've done my best, but it's the other person's problem."

To declare this does not mean we stop praying for the one who hurt us. Yet instead of running scared, interceding out of a weakened capacity, we pray with a release in our spirit that commits the person and situation totally to the Lord. Our attitude reflects one woman's comment, "It's *God's* problem."

Christ walked a balance between silence and spunk. At his trial he spoke little before his accusers, but earlier, when money changers made a sacrilege of his Father's house, he overturned tables and drove them out. His actions said, "That's enough. I will not accept your behavior."

As we come before God, evaluating our own circumstances, we have to decide which behavior is appropriate—silence or spunk. After experiencing two tension-related diseases, one of them life-threatening, I had enough of the money changers. I brought before the Lord those people who consistently took advantage of my need to be loved and approved, and I prayed, "Jesus, I'm tired of being physically ill because I can't handle what they do to me. I commit myself to love and pray for them—to give help if they want my help. Yet give me the ability to see their behavior in balance."

As a college freshman put it, "I refuse to let the flaming arrows soak in, spreading poison. The problem isn't necessarily me, even though cruel comments are directed at me."

The long view

When their herdsmen argued over water rights, Abraham relinquished first choice and allowed Lot to pick the best. Seemingly Abraham lost out, yet after Lot left, God renewed his promise of blessing (Gen. 13:14-17).

Forgiveness should not be mistaken for passivity. When we forgive and seek workable solutions with others, we receive a blood transfusion—new life and strength for coping with our situation. Our ultimate encouragement comes from the Lord.

Again, think about Leah. Though her need to be loved was

not filled by Jacob, she had another resource—God the Father. When he saw she was not loved, he opened her womb. To three sons she gave names acknowledging that situation and hoping her husband would love her. But there was no change. When a fourth son arrived, Leah named him *Judah,* saying, "This time I will praise the Lord" (Gen. 29:35). From that son came the line of descent out of which Jesus Christ was born.

Like Leah, we may have instances in our life where we do not understand why we must continue to experience hurt. Yet God can give us the ability to trust without sight in his long view. Cruel Pharisees brought a necessary dimension into Christ's life so that he fulfilled his work for eternity. So, too, can the Holy Spirit develop in us a Christ-like quality: "Therefore have I set my face like flint, and I know I will not be put to shame" (Isa. 50:7).

Often healing accelerates when we sense the need of another. Or perhaps that is the first sign of healing—to be able to see a greater hurt or injustice. When I desperately needed to know I was worthy of love, I saw God the Father with new insight.

"Lois," came that quiet understanding, "have you ever thought about all the moments in which I have been rejected? All the times I have loved people, and they didn't love me? All the ways I have blessed them, and they wanted my gifts instead of me? Yet I loved them so unconditionally that I sent my only Son. And they killed him. They *killed* him! But I'm still waiting. I still love them. I still forgive all those who come to me."

He never wastes pain.

11 *What do your scars indicate?*

Exchange Your Wounds for Self-Esteem

A dark-eyed, attractive young woman posed a question many had been afraid to ask: "How did you deal with the scar from your mastectomy?"

I can't remember my response, but it was immediate and from the heart. To me the world is a place full of scars—reminders of lives that have been changed.

As I thought about her question, I realized the potential power of any wound—physical, emotional, or spiritual. If unhealed, an injury permanently affects self-esteem. If, instead, a wound heals properly, there may be a mark, but the scar indicates progress. The individual has grown.

How might the choice of healing be ours? Can we develop attitudes of self-esteem grounded in Jesus Christ? Let's consider, first of all, how to deal with existing wounds.

Something causing emotional upset can heal in one big positive happening, but more often it involves a gradual process. Leaving injuries behind requires time alone in which we face and work through the situations causing hurt.

I remember the first bath after my mastectomy, when my incision was still an angry red line. The nurse left the room, and I was glad, for I needed to be alone to face what had happened. In that moment I knew that many friends were praying, for I sensed the supportive love of the Holy Spirit. I pushed back tears, thinking, *If it isn't worse than this, I can make it.*

But then I returned home from the hospital, and a woman came to visit. Though meaning well, her appraising eyes gave away her thoughts. After she left, I went into my bedroom, and this time tears came in a flood. Finally, I blew my nose and realized I would have to get used to such treatment. From past experience I knew there can be no self-esteem without forgiveness. Though my emotions fought against it, I prayed the John 20:23 prayer: "Jesus, in your name, I forgive her. I ask you to bless her." Two weeks later, I discovered with surprise that I no longer felt pain when confronted by that kind of situation. God's healing was real.

When we experience emotional pain, our feelings aren't neatly packaged and in order. At those times it is essential to remember that you and I forgive with the will. It helps me to imagine Jesus standing next to the person who hurt me, for it is difficult to be angry with someone in his presence.

Even as forgiveness is necessary for self-esteem, so is the knowledge that we are loved. We all enjoy the *sense* of being loved, but the *knowledge* of being loved is even more important. After offering the John 20:23 prayer, I pray, "Jesus, I ask in your name for healing. Bind up all the ragged edges, bringing wholeness to me and to the other person. Pour through us with your Spirit's love, restoring self-esteem. Thank you." Often God responds by giving an immediate sense of well-being. Other times I find my self-esteem returning as I lay hold of such promises as the one given through Jeremiah: "I will restore health to you, and your wounds I will heal" (30:17 RSV).

The Holy Spirit uses our willingness to offer such prayers, whether they involve recent injuries or long-standing ones.

Often self-worth grows, or fails to germinate, according to our roots and the watering we enjoy. As young children, we need parents, siblings, teachers, and friends who encourage us, helping develop self-esteem. Each time we face and surmount a new experience, we learn to adapt to changing life situations. As we mature, we need continuing positive experiences and the sense of being loved and respected. Like a flower opening to sunlight, we open ourselves to warmth and affirmation.

But what if we didn't receive that encouragement? Will we be plants lying in the dirt, never rising to our potential? Too often we place the blame for our problems on others and their failures. Instead, we need to seek the Lord and his power to heal whatever happened in the past.

"Jesus Christ is the same yesterday and today and forever" (Heb. 13:8). He was present at those times when you and I desperately needed encouragement and didn't receive it. Years later, he brings wholeness if we forgive the persons who hurt us.

Once we have forgiven others, we come to the hardest part —forgiving ourselves. Again, it is accomplished with the will. One day I realized I had to relinquish my feelings about my appearance. I thought of Jesus and his scars—in his hands, his feet, his side. Weren't those scars for me?

Then I prayed, "Jesus, in your name I forgive myself for the way I look." The Holy Spirit blessed that prayer, and I never again felt the same about my scar. In some intangible way it became a mark of battle. Yes, I had been wounded, but I was alive. Yes, I had been hurt, but in Jesus Christ I had grown.

Once we have experienced healing for existing wounds, how might we receive ongoing care?

Those of us who are deeply sensitive pick up hurts like a fuzz ball rolling down a dusty hall. We are called to see and respond with empathy to the needs of others. Yet if overly sensitive, we swing out of balance and consistently live in hurt. One day I realized how such feelings hinder my Christian witness, always making me feel defeated. When I asked, "Jesus, in your name, heal me from acute sensitivity," I sensed the burden of countless hurts leaving instantly.

For some time, I noticed that things which normally would have hurt me just rolled off. Through the power of the Holy Spirit, I could handle them. When I started once more to accumulate hurt, I sought the Lord. Again he helped me, causing me to form new patterns of thinking.

When we have dealt with past wounds or negative attitudes, we need to meet daily each new and threatening battle. We cannot wait for the flaming arrows of unthinking comments or real and pointed remarks to spread poison. Nor can we continually receive and take into ourselves thoughts and suggestions that are not of the Lord.

If we have a physical wound, we take precautions to keep dirt out of it. We don't want infection. In the same way, spiritual dirt weakens us and affects self-esteem. While attending a short course at a university, I read some obscene graffiti. I felt dirty, and knew the words would linger with me. In that moment the Holy Spirit taught me a prayer. "Lord, cleanse my mind. I don't want to remember that."

But it's not enough to just pray against negative or filthy thoughts. We have to replace them with something better. A healthy self-image flows from a clean body and a clean mind. As Paul said, "Whatever is true, whatever is noble, whatever is right, whatever is pure, whatever is lovely, whatever is admirable—if anything is excellent or praiseworthy—*think* about such things" (Phil. 4:8).

In crucial times I want the bank of my mind filled to overflowing with promises I can withdraw as necessary. A thought from Psalm 84, for instance: "I am the dwelling place of the Lord. I am lovely." Or from Psalm 45, "The king is enthralled by your beauty; honor him, for he is your lord" (v. 11).

As a public school teacher, my husband needs strong self-esteem. It's a matter of survival. One Christmas vacation our family traveled from frigid Minnesota to Texas and the Gulf of Mexico. Eighty-degree weather greeted us, along with a seemingly endless strip of beach. Our toes dug into the sand, the sun warmed our shoulders, and the waves reached out to play tag. As the end of our time neared, Roy and I strolled hand in hand, speaking of our return to below zero cold and great heaps of snow. "This is what I'll remember," he said. "When the winter becomes long and my class gets hard, this is what I'll remember."

After my mastectomy, I was grateful I had developed many reasons for which to live—my family, work, relationships with others. But I was also deeply aware that beauty is Spirit-deep. There is an inner beauty given only to those who seek God: "And we, who with unveiled faces all reflect the Lord's glory, are being transformed into his likeness with ever-increasing glory, which comes from the Lord, who is the Spirit" (2 Cor. 3:18). Those with such a glow have a loveliness greater than any possible physical beauty.

Whoever we are, with great or limited resources, we need to make and bank memories ready for any need—investments of our King's treasury.

If we would exchange our wounds for self-esteem, we may also need to swallow some strong medicine. Take, for instance, the problem of comparing ourselves or our achievements with those of others. Perhaps you're like me. Struggle as I might against it, I usually compare my weaknesses with another's strengths. Of course, I always come up wanting.

One of my friends has a slightly different problem: "I feel I need to be perfect. I compare myself with what I think I should be. When someone says, 'You did great!' I answer, 'I only did 95 percent. I failed, because it wasn't 100.'"

That isn't the humility Scripture encourages us to have. Our striving comes out of an insecure feeling about self. For a long time I struggled with feelings of perfectionism and worthlessness. Then one day the Holy Spirit showed me I actually suffered from pride. What if others didn't think well enough of me? Each time such feelings return, I try to remember to confess them as sin, and ask the Lord for the ability to do the best I can—no more, but no less.

All of us need identities. Sometimes we need the control of those identities in order to be an effective wife, mother, or single person. When we identify ourselves as persons who persevere, we keep on, even when it's tough. We finish a project we dislike because it needs to be finished.

Yet there's a truth essential to self-esteem: *you and I have value apart from our functional identity.* Often it appears that loved ones, and especially any children we may have, love us only for what we do for them. When I was hospitalized and for a time unable to work, I found that my family loved me anyway. So, too, does God. He's not going to love you and me less because we're laid off from a job, or unable to produce as much as we once did. He loves us as persons—just exactly the way we are. Always he says, "I have loved you with an everlasting love; I have drawn you with loving-kindness" (Jer. 31:3).

Think of a growing child within a family. Do the parents love that child because of the small tasks he or she completes? Or because the child is a person of value to them?

But aside from our ability to work, what if we base the way we feel about ourselves *solely* on the actions or responses of others? Both their feelings and ours change according to circumstances. If such circumstances are positive, we see ourselves in a positive light. If negative, we see ourselves negatively. When we are tired or discouraged, we put ourselves down, and lose even more hope.

"God is the only one who never changes in the depth of his commitment to me," said one woman. On a day of deep need, I discovered Christ's prayer to his Father about those yet to believe: "You . . . have loved them even as you have loved me" (John 17:23). Jesus freely recognized that God cherishes you and me just as much as he cherishes his only Son. Jesus is not the jealous big brother.

Yet do we truly believe what God the Father and God the Son said? Or are we so busy looking at our wounds that we do not give the Lord a chance to exchange them for self-worth? I feel sure he would rather have us looking at him, instead of continually gazing inward.

In her book *Out of My Heart,* Agnes Sligh Turnbull speaks of a line written by Solomon, King of Israel: "The spirit of man is the candle of the Lord." She writes: "I took this at once at its face value without reading farther. No matter what the great wise man had in his mind, here was a thought for which I had been waiting, and which suggested a new slant to all my thinking. Suppose that man's spirit could actually afford *light* to God himself!" (p. 8).

Suppose we are important to him! That is the secret of praise and adoration. We offer the Lord light each time we appreciate him for being who he is. As we worship him, all else falls away. We catch a glimpse of his majesty, glory, and kingship. We grow in the realization that Jesus loves us unconditionally and without reservation. Whether we *feel* that love is not important. We *know* the promise: "The eyes of the Lord range throughout the earth to strengthen those whose hearts are fully committed to him" (2 Chron. 16:9).

Because of an accumulation of experiences in which my sense of self-worth self-destructed, I asked my pastor to pray for me. After his prayer, I wrote down these words so I can remember them: "My worth is not dependent on whether I am accepted or rejected. Nor does it depend on whether I succeed or fail. My worth is not even dependent on the love of other human beings. I have worth because I am forgiven by Jesus Christ and loved by him. *The ground at the foot of the cross is level.*"

Because of that cross, Jesus stands with arms outstretched, welcoming each of us. His scars are proof that something happened. They affirm our greatest gift—forgiveness and eternal life. But they also remind us that he knows what it means to suffer. He will keep his promise: "All whom My Father has given (entrusted) to Me will come to Me; and him who comes to Me I will certainly not cast out—I will never, no never reject one of them who comes to Me" (John 6:37 Amplified Bible).

Whatever wound needs to be exchanged for self-esteem, you and I are unconditionally important to Jesus. The ground at the foot of the cross is level.

12

Seldom, if ever, does loneliness enter a life by itself. It seems afraid to come alone, and appears with an ever-changing array of mates offering debris.

Four Ways to Defeat Loneliness

Fear not, for I am with you, says the Lord (Isa. 41:10). Fear not. Bold words are those, and ones of promise, for who among us likes to be lonely? Considered a symptom of singles, loneliness is, instead, a disease that plagues everyone, young and old alike.

Most of us dread that illness, and with good reason. Our need to be loved is one of the most basic of all human needs. We don't even like to admit we are lonely, for in some not-always-logical way, it seems we have failed. We don't cherish the emptiness that continually hopes a special person will be around the corner—in the next room we enter, or the next hall through which we pass. It hurts to ache for a loved one separated from us by distance. Even more painful is the anguish that follows death. We sense we are cut in two, with the open side exposed and bleeding.

Loneliness makes us feel we are falling apart. Or if we are falling apart for other reasons, we often feel lonely—set aside by everyone. No one understands.

Yet what does the Lord say? Fear not. Don't be afraid, even of loneliness. "*Fear not, for I have redeemed you; I have called you by name; you are mine*" (Isa. 43:1; see vv. 1-3).

How can we know without doubt we are his? Whatever the cause—an empty nest, singleness, death of a loved one, an unequally yoked marriage, feeling set apart in a nonbelieving world—there are certain principles that remain the same. How can we experience God's faithfulness?

First of all, we need to believe that the Lord wants the best for us. That need goes all the way back to the Garden. The serpent came to the woman, asking, "Did God *really* say, 'You must not eat from any tree in the garden'?" Eve saw the fruit of the tree was good for food, pleasing to the eye, and desirable for gaining wisdom. She decided she knew better than God, took the fruit, and ate of it. How could he possibly desire the best for her? (Gen. 3:1-7).

For each of us God stands ready to offer his assurance of love: *I have called you by name, you are mine.* Yet you and I ask, "Did God really say that about *me?*"

Out of the trillions of people who have lived, the countless masses now living, and the unnumbered throng yet to live, God knows each of us by name. He says, *You are mine.* When the threat of loneliness tempts us to doubt that, we can remind ourselves, "In spite of the way I feel, I am his; however others treat me, I am his; though a seeming failure, I am his." God loves you and me in such individual ways that he remembers us by name.

At times I feel lonely because of my unwillingness to accept the Lord's timing: I want what I want when I want it. Or I need to adjust to the seasons of life. Yet often loneliness comes for much deeper reasons.

Ione's husband Fred died suddenly of a heart attack at the age of 52. Shortly before, she sensed the Spirit's warning: "Come to me, all who labor and are heavy laden, and I will give you rest. Take my yoke upon you, and learn from me;

for I am gentle and lowly in heart, and you will find rest for your souls" (Matt. 11:28-29 RSV).

Ione acknowledged the difference the power of the Holy Spirit makes: "The Lord prepared me. Certainly it's not what I would have chosen, but that Scripture helped me sense God in everything. After Fred died, I went back to those verses and knew the Lord was going to take care of me. He has. I really believe this is his best for me."

She looked back over the five years of her widowhood. "God has protected me. Only once have I known that terrible, deep loneliness. Soon after Fred's death I woke up terror-stricken, thinking, "I'm all alone in the whole world." I got my Bible, but I couldn't even read. I just hung on to it until I went to sleep."

Most of us know that helpless feeling when loneliness washes over us at the mere thought of a loved one. Ione referred to a recent Sunday morning when she dissolved into tears. "Yes, I miss my husband. When I see other couples planning a nice trip, I think, 'For me that chapter won't be written.' When I hear a wife complain about her husband, I think, 'How can you do that? You *have* him.' But except for that one time, I have never felt truly alone. The Lord always sends someone on bad days. It's good to know that, and to look for those people who will be there."

Second, we experience the Lord's faithfulness as we choose between being overwhelmed by circumstances and looking to God. He reassures us, *When you pass through the waters I will be with you.*

Before we were married, my husband was a widower. Afraid at one point that he would also lose me, he had a nightmare in which he began to weep. As he woke up, he seemed to be drowning in tears.

It is not unusual to fear loneliness, especially when we have experienced great loss. But we must face it honestly, rather than trying to escape into oblivion. When our fear of drowning

107

is more than we can handle, how can we *know* God will take us through?

When I was 10 years old we moved to another state. I didn't want to make new friends, thinking that soon we would move again and I would leave those friends also. Not until years later did I discover that every friend made enlarges our experience, changing to a greater or lesser degree the person we are. In essence, I was telling myself something on which many of us dwell: "I don't *feel* loved."

The feeling of being loved is crucial to our well-being. Yet if we base our Christian life and our knowledge of being loved solely on feelings, those feelings become huge waves. The moment we feel defeated or lonely, we look at those waves and stumble into a drop-off. No longer are we loved—or so it seems.

What is God's solution? He encourages us to walk on water. When we look to Jesus and the promises of Scripture, we receive the Holy Spirit's ability to live by faith. We find Jesus greater than outward circumstances. As one young man put it, "There have been times when I have been lonely, and the Holy Spirit reminded me, 'Why don't you spend some time with me?' "

One of the most important secrets of the Christian life involves building on God's promises, instead of on feelings. We do so by choosing with our will to open the Bible and begin reading. If we allow him, the Holy Spirit helps us make that choice. Then God blesses our desire to depend on him. At the right time he brings our emotions into line.

We may have to decide, "It takes too much energy to keep on crying. I'm going to get back to the business of living." Ione put it this way: "Dealing with loneliness is deciding you will not be lonely. After my husband died, I used to say, 'I'll go to the nursing home and talk with someone.' I set my mind to seeking out others and helping them. It doesn't work to be introspective and wait for people to come to you. It's necessary to set your will to not let loneliness take over."

While we use our will to counteract what we do about being lonely, everyone who has experienced grief knows that we cannot control the intense aching for someone simply by willing to be happy. All it takes is one poignant reminder of our loved one, and we begin to weep. What part does the will play in this kind of anguish? In *Beyond Our Selves* Catherine Marshall explains:

> The secret—Hannah Smith's secret—is simple recognition of the fact that sorrow is an emotion and that you have little control over it. You know that God loves your loved one, who is now with Him, and that He loves you. You know that God has a plan for your life. So you admit to God that you are divided. One part of you is clinging to grief almost as an indulgence; another part knows well that until you are willing to let grief go, happiness and a good life cannot be yours again.
>
> The principle of the will can handle this division, though we have to begin farther back. Our prayer here must be, "Lord, I am willing to be made willing."
>
> And there one lets the matter rest for days or weeks, doing no forcing or straining, giving God time to change the emotional climate at deep levels in the personality (pp. 77-78).

As we look to God instead of the circumstances of loneliness, he again speaks in love: *When you pass through the waters I will be with you; and through the rivers, they shall not overwhelm you.*

In the spring of the year most rivers are full. If snow melts suddenly, or if early rains are long and steady, it can mean disaster. A river rampages out of its banks. All that is assailable, all that can be broken or torn loose, all that is near-at-hand meets a common fate—the angry, roiling water. Wherever the river flows, it deposits its accumulation of dirt and debris.

In times of loneliness we experience God's faithfulness in a third way if we understand that he gives the power to leave debris behind. We might think of our life as a riverbank. From the beginning of our days to the end a great many experiences flow through. We have control over some; over others we do not. If our life is winding and circuitous, it offers frequent places for debris to catch.

Seldom, if ever, does only loneliness enter a life. It seems afraid to come alone, and appears with an ever-changing array of mates offering debris: rejection, guilt, bitterness, complaining, resentment, or unforgiveness. But there's one companion loneliness seems to like best of all—self-pity. What could possibly ravage the banks of our life more than the debris of self-pity?

Through a combination of circumstances in her marital life, there was a long period of time in which Sharon went to church alone. She described her reaction: "It became a spiritual battleground. Feeling like a lost sparrow, I'd huddle in the corner of a pew while Satan whispered, 'Here you are again, all alone. Too bad. Look at all the happy people around you who have family and friends.'

"Soon it didn't do me much good to attend church. I couldn't hear the pastor speaking, or the reading of Scripture. Trying to hide my feelings, I'd wipe away a tear, then spend the remaining time holding more back. Even if I succeeded in maintaining outward self-control, I nearly drowned in my inward pity party. So caught up was I in my problems and feelings that it took me a long time to gain insight into what was really happening."

Like Sharon, many of us find that Satan becomes effective when he shifts our point of view. We look inward instead of God-ward. In *My Utmost for His Highest,* Oswald Chambers says, "No sin is worse than the sin of self-pity, because it obliterates God and puts self-interest upon the throne."

When Sharon confessed her attitude of self-pity as sin, she realized she was living in her emotions instead of letting God do something about the situation. The next time Satan spoke to her about loneliness, she resisted his whisper, praying with her will: "Lord, thank you that I'm here alone today—that because of it I can give you my undivided attention. Thank you that I can better sense the hurt of single, or divorced, or widowed women, and give them a hug. I praise you!" Each time Satan returned with his lie, she immediately offered a similar prayer.

The story doesn't end there. One by one, over a period of years, the members of Sharon's family joined her in the pew.

As we receive the Holy Spirit's power to leave debris behind, he reminds us, *When you walk through fire you shall not be burned, and the flame shall not consume you.* In a fourth way, God faithfully encourages us. If we allow him, he rescues us from the fire of temptation, turning our loneliness into productive aloneness.

Temptation offers potential for the greatest loneliness of all—separation from the love of God. We are most vulnerable to any kind of temptation when we feel set apart.

A woman who has been through divorce said, "Sexual compromise is one of the biggest temptations for a single person. Many say, 'This is the point where I put God off. The loneliness for someone present seems greater than the reality of an invisible God.' Often someone tells me, 'I love God, but I just want someone close to me with skin on.' Most people in the fire of temptation will compromise. Instead of compromising, we need to stand alone."

Here again, God is faithful, no matter what form temptation takes. On the cross his Son carried our sin, knowing a separation from God's holiness out of which he cried, "My God, my God, why have you forsaken me?" Because of his death, resurrection, and sending of the Holy Spirit, we have access to the power that turns temptation into a test, strengthening us.

How many great men and women of God have known the fire of standing on their convictions? Did they cry out in despair, "I don't like being lonely"? Did they hear Jesus say, "I know; I too walked alone"? And did they come to the triumph of productive aloneness?

Those persons God truly uses go beyond their natural human need to be loved and approved, unwilling to compromise God's righteousness. How better can we follow our Savior? If we stand firm, God uses our time of aloneness as a refining fire. He burns from us all that would hinder our commitment to him.

A friend of mine reminds singles of additional benefits: "Consider this time of aloneness not a period, but a comma. Use this comma in your life to do something constructive. Take up a hobby. Read. Travel. Learn something new. Don't waste this time, but use it to grow and develop as a person."

When you and I allow God to change our loneliness into productive aloneness, we hear his words: *For I am the Lord your God, the Holy One of Israel, your Savior.* He calls us to be "a chosen people, a royal priesthood, a holy nation, a people belonging to God." Why? That we may declare the praises of the one who called us out of darkness into his light (1 Peter 2:9). In that giving of praises from the depths of our spirit we *know* we are not alone. We call him Savior, Lord, King, Master, and Friend. He responds: *Fear not, I am with you. . . . I have called you by name, you are mine.*

In times of loneliness I have often begun to sing. If not with my emotions, then with my will. God never fails to bless my desire to worship him. He brings me to an attitude of productive aloneness.

Adjusting to a new culture, thousands of miles from home, a young man realized an ocean separated him from everyone he deeply loved. In his loneliness he came to this conclusion: "While working for God is important, God has shown me anew to seek *him*—that *he* is who I need—not a more comfortable life-style, or my friends and family back home. When I woke up this morning the first thing that entered my mind was 'Another awful day!' But I put that behind me and remembered, 'O Lord, I have *you*, king of the universe and the living God, even if I have nothing else.' 'Whom have I in heaven *but Thee?* And besides Thee, I desire nothing on earth. My flesh and my heart may fail, but God is the strength of my heart and my portion forever'" (Ps. 73:25-26 NAS).

When we dwell in loneliness, life seems as drab as the end of winter: brown, matted grass, dead leaves still tucked in crevices, debris left behind as snow melts out from beneath it. But when the Spirit begins our healing, the hint of green grass appears, followed by the reality. Above the gray trunks

112

of maples appear buds that from a distance seem rose-colored masses. Unmasked by green or gold leaves, birch shine brilliant white, and lofty pines, just washed by rain, a velvet green.

That's the beginning, the edging out of loneliness into the aloneness in which we welcome the presence of God. Occasionally spring comes overnight; more often gradually. Yet with the gradual, we have additional time to savor its arrival.

13 *As we grow in our prayer life, we dare to ask difficult things from the Father who is also ruler of the universe.*

Key Thoughts for Power-Packed Prayer

In May 1948, the United Nations asked Folke Bernadotte to mediate between the Arabs and Jews in Palestine. To the entire world the mission appeared hopeless. It was also potentially dangerous. Yet Bernadotte believed a person should not undertake only easy tasks. With courage he accepted the challenge, and during his first month as mediator accomplished the seemingly impossible. On June 11th he announced a truce that offered a breathing space for further negotiations.

A reporter asked how he had achieved the armistice, and Bernadotte replied: "My father [Prince Oscar] away back home is more than 80 years of age. When I came out here on this job, he gave me a new Bible. And he promised every day to remember me in his prayers. He is not alone. Thousands of Christians have promised to beseech God on my behalf. It is my conviction that without God's help and support this result would never have come about."

Too often you and I look only at the circumstances in today's world or our own life. Those circumstances may seem hopeless —at times even dangerous. Like Folke Bernadotte, we enter a battle, well aware of the high cost of victory. Yet God makes provision for bringing change. To each of us he offers the resource of prayer, the intercession through which we stand before him on behalf of someone or something.

With each reason for falling apart, there is at least one reason—often several—for which we need to pray effectively. We might ask, "What key thoughts will help me offer power-packed prayer?"

Relationship

As one of five growing up in a home operating under a stringent budget, I had the right to ask, "Daddy, can I get new shoes for school?" Because of World War II, shoes were rationed, yet my father did his best, not only to buy shoes of good quality, but also ones that I liked.

Our heavenly Father is much the same. He knows our needs, and separates them from wants that would hinder our growth. Talking with him is as simple as crawling onto the lap of a cherished earthly father. In such moments we realize we don't have to be a supersaint in order to pray. We live out the meaning of Hallesby's words: "Prayer and helplessness are inseparable. Only he who is helpless can truly pray."

A sense of the Father's love is an important preparation for effective prayer. Through that love, he shows us how to ask and makes us aware of the prayers he delights in answering. The deeper our understanding of his love for us, the more eager we are to pray. Prayer *is* the language of a relationship.

We experience prayer power in direct proportion to the degree in which we rely on God. Only then can we see something as he sees it. Only then do we regard sin for what it is— an offense to God's holiness. Only then do we learn to abide, to rest in Jesus Christ, receiving the promise, "If you remain in me and my words remain in you, ask whatever you wish, and it will be given you" (John 15:7).

Specific heart's desire

Blind Bartimaeus called out, "Jesus, Son of David, have mercy on me!" When people told him to be quiet he shouted again, "Son of David, have mercy on me!"

Bartimaeus expected something to happen. No doubt Jesus knew what he needed, but he encouraged him to ask specifically:

"What do you want me to do for you?"

The blind man replied, "Rabbi, I want to see."

"Go," said Jesus, "your faith has healed you" (Mark 10:46-52).

When we use the amount of faith we have, God gives us more. The first book of Samuel tells about an ordinary woman named Hannah who suffered under the treatment of her husband's other wife. Hannah's honest need to present her husband with an heir became a deep desire.

The psalmist talks about such a motivation: "Delight yourself in the Lord and he will give you the desires of your heart. Commit your way to the Lord; trust in him and he will do this" (37:4-5). The first part of the verse, "Delight yourself," reminds us of the importance of a praise-filled spirit. That comes first. Committing ourselves to the Lord, trusting him fully, is also part of the package. But what about the deep desires of our heart?

Bible teacher Ken Chant talked about the motivation of a deep desire, referring to Ps. 81:10-16. There God reminds his people of his caring nature: "I am the Lord your God, who brought you up out of Egypt. Open wide your mouth and I will fill it." Then we sense the grieving in his voice: "But my people would not listen to me; Israel would not submit to me. So I gave them over to their stubborn hearts to follow their own devices."

God wanted to give abundance, but his idolatrous people refused it. After a long insistence on their own way, God finally gave them what they actually wanted. The nation reaped the misery of its own choice.

Chant explained: "God will give you what you really want—whether heaven or hell, righteousness or sin."

For a long time I prayed about someone's attitude toward me before I heard the gentle voice of the Spirit: "What is it you really want, Lois? Your motives are mixed. Be honest before God about how you really feel about your situation."

What is it that I really want? Out of Hannah's deep desire sprang Samuel's birth. Eventually recognized as a prophet, priest, and intercessor, he had historical importance in the sight of God and others. He pulled Israel together at a time when disintegration threatened the nation, becoming its second founder.[1]

A cleansed heart

The psalmist makes it very clear: "If I had cherished sin in my heart, the Lord would not have listened" (66:18). When Solomon dedicated the temple, the Lord appeared to him in the middle of the night, offering both a promise and a warning: "When I shut up the heavens so that there is no rain, or command locusts to devour the land or send a plague among my people, if my people, who are called by my name, will humble themselves and pray and seek my face and turn from their wicked ways, then will I hear from heaven and will forgive their sin and will heal their land" (2 Chron. 7:13-14).

Readiness for battle

If only those who are helpless can truly pray, why do we need to be equipped for battle? When you and I discover the simplicity and the joy of prayer within a loving relationship, we lay hold of a power that threatens Satan. He recognizes that power as one through which kingdoms can be changed. He knows that as we grow in our prayer life, we dare to ask difficult things from the Father who is also ruler of the universe. He doesn't want that to happen.

No soldier who values his life enters a war zone without knowing where the battle is waged. A Christian's battle takes place in the spiritual realm, for Paul warns, "Our struggle is not against flesh and blood, but against the rulers, against the authorities, against the powers of this dark world and against the spiritual forces of evil in the heavenly realms."

---

1. See 1 Sam. 3:19-20; 7:2-10; 12:23; Ps. 99:6; Jer. 15:1.

Paul also tells us what to do about the situation: "Therefore put on the full armor of God, so that when the day of evil comes, you may be able to stand your ground, and after you have done everything, to stand" (Eph. 6:12-13).

If we wish to stand firm in prayer, we need to allow God to deal with our will, bringing us to that point of brokenness where we are dependent on him. Out of brokenness we know the difference between human stubbornness and divine. The first insists on what we want. The second is a God-given perseverance that places us in the front lines of a battle from which we dare not retreat.

Before entering a spiritual war, we have the privilege of putting on the armor suggested by Paul. Each piece covers a specific area of vulnerability—sexual, emotional, intellectual, or spiritual. (To pray on this armor, see Eph. 6:14-18.)

God's authority

A Roman centurion came to Jesus, asking for help: "Lord, my servant lies at home paralyzed and in terrible suffering."

"Jesus said to him, 'I will go and heal him.'

"The centurion replied, 'Lord, I do not deserve to have you come under my roof. But just say the word, and my servant will be healed. For I myself am a man under authority, with soldiers under me. I tell this one, "Go," and he goes; and that one, "Come," and he comes. I say to my servant, "Do this," and he does it.' "

Jesus was amazed and responded, " 'I tell you the truth, I have not found anyone in Israel with such great faith. . . . Go! It will be done just as you believed it would.' " The servant was healed that very hour (Matt. 8:5-13).

If you sense a need for authority, ask the Holy Spirit to show you scriptural principles and examples in that area. The Spirit wants us to see all that Jesus can do. At first our steps may be hesitant, even as Peter's upon the water. Yet each time we immerse ourselves in Scripture, then depend wholeheartedly on the Lord, you and I grow in the boldness of prayer. We realize, like the centurion, that Jesus is a man of authority.

He never claimed to have authority in his own right. It was given to him (Matt. 28:18-19). Even as the Father gave authority to Jesus, so Jesus gave authority to his disciples. Calling the Twelve together, he "gave them power and authority to drive out all demons and to cure diseases, and he sent them out to preach the kingdom of God and to heal the sick" (Luke 9:1-2). Out of that same authority, he appointed 72 others and sent them out two-by-two. When they returned, overflowing with excitement about all that had happened, he replied, "I saw Satan fall like lightning from heaven. I have given you authority to trample on snakes and scorpions, and to overcome all the power of the enemy; nothing will harm you" (10:18-19).

Authority is given in the moment we need it, for those needs about which God wants us to pray. Most often it seems he expects us to pray about those portions of Ezekiel's wall right in front of us (Ezek. 22:30).

The power for any prayer rests in the name of Jesus. For three years I suffered from a deep emotional wound. I went through the stages of grief, forgave, asked forgiveness, received counseling from two pastors, and thought I had taken care of everything. Even so, whenever I remembered the circumstances, I felt pain as though a knife turned within.

At God's chosen time, he brought a third pastor into my life. As he prayed, he said, "Don't think of me. Don't think of the circumstances, think of the name of Jesus."

In that moment I saw the word *Jesus* in bold, black letters. Within the outline of the letters twinkled countless small lights. Behind the word another light glowed, as I spoke the name of Jesus.

Even now, I remember all the circumstances of the incident from which I suffered. Yet whenever I think about the situation, I feel no pain. Only peace.

The mind of God

The Lord desires a thankful, praise-filled spirit. Through Paul he tells us to thank him even as we ask: "Do not be anxious about anything, but in everything, by prayer and petition, *with thanksgiving*, present your requests to God" (Phil. 4:6).

To do battle through effective prayer, it is essential that we know the mind of God. Often I hear people pray, "If it is your will, bring my loved one to salvation." It is *always* God's will that someone comes to salvation: "The Lord is not slow in keeping his promise, as some understand slowness. He is patient with you, not wanting anyone to perish, but *everyone* to come to repentance" (2 Peter 3:9; italics added).

It is also God's will that every person live in the full power of the Holy Spirit. Jesus told his disciples, " 'I am going to send you what my Father has promised; but stay in the city until you have been clothed with power from on high" (Luke 24:49).

In these two areas in particular we ask in the assurance that we *always* know what God wants. Therefore it is wise to pray against the hardness of heart that prevents many from coming into God's joy and power.

For some prayer situations God leads us step-by-step. As we see one prayer being answered, the Spirit prompts us to give thanks, then leads us on to another prayer. For this reason it is often necessary to ask, "Lord, how do you want me to pray?" The Spirit of prayer will show us.

Scripture-based prayers

One evening I visited with friends who had endured a four-year battle with organized crime. Because the husband refused to give in to Mafia demands, he and his wife lost their home, their cars, and their business. Three attempts were made on his life. A short time before, he had been arrested and jailed for a crime he did not commit. Facing the threat of long-term imprisonment, he knew it would be almost impossible to receive a fair trial.

The three of us talked and prayed together about Paul's guideline for dealing with enemies: "Do not take revenge, my friends, but leave room for God's wrath, for it is written: 'It is mine to avenge; I will repay,' says the Lord" (Rom. 12:19).

Feeling totally drained, I then drove to an intercessory group at our church. Coming in late, I found the others offering prayers of adoration, confession, and thanksgiving. In that moment in which I felt I could not pray, God used their Scripture-based sentences to give me courage, as well as suggest new ways of interceding for the battered family I had left behind.

"Lord, you have the government on your shoulders," said one woman, and I thought, "A fair trial, Lord." On the other side of the circle a man prayed, "You spoke, and it came to be." Silently I added, "You *will* speak, and the money they need will come into being." Then our pastor said, "The fear of the Lord is to hate evil." I began hating the evil of organized crime, and praying against it. (See Isa. 9:6; Genesis 1; Prov. 8:13.)

Moments later, we stopped and agreed how to pray about the situation, but already God had begun to work in our group. In time he answered by providing a fair trial and acquittal.

Willingness to persevere

Jesus offers a pattern for different kinds of prayer: " 'Ask and it will be given to you' " (an answer comes immediately, often after one prayer); " 'seek and you will find' " (pray a bit harder against obstacles); " 'knock and the door will be opened to you' " (pound on the door of heaven) (Matt. 7:7). Knocking requires the perseverance shown by the persistent widow, used as an example by Jesus for praying without giving up (Luke 18:1-8). We may need to pray until we sense a release of peace.

We persevere, not against God, but *against* evil, and *for* someone or something. That perseverance may involve fasting, which requires both spiritual and physical commitment. Jesus and his disciples considered this more intensive prayer a normal part of the God-directed life and a foundation for ministry (Matt. 4:1-2; Acts 13:2-3). God tells us that the kind of fasting which pleases him will "set the oppressed free and break every yoke" (Isa. 58:6).[1]

A few ideas will help you with the physical aspects. When not fasting, maintain a balanced diet, including whole grains, fresh fruits, and vegetables. Then, to avoid discouragement, start by omitting just one meal or two. Gradually increase the time, perhaps setting aside a certain day each week. If the Spirit so leads, go on a three-day or longer fast.

Some individuals drink only water during a fast; others take skim milk, broth, and juice. Scripture reveals that some fasts omitted fluids. However, *do not go* without fluids longer than the 72 hours undertaken by Esther. (If diabetic or under other medical care, consult a doctor before attempting *any* fast.)

Have in mind specific prayer concerns or goals. Write them down. Read Scripture as much as possible. You may wish to pray in secret (Matt. 6:16-18), or to agree with others on important needs (Matt. 18:19-20). At first you may feel that all you can think about is your hunger. With experience you will begin seeing the benefits of fasting and sense a deepened ability to hear God speak.

Ability to wait

Hallesby writes, "The more completely you cease being concerned about the time in which your prayers are to be answered, the more freedom you will enjoy in your prayer life."

When Abram was 75 years old God gave him a command and a promise: "Leave your country, your people and your father's household and go to the land I will show you. I will make you into a great nation and I will bless you; I will make your name great, and you will be a blessing. . . . all peoples on earth will be blessed through you" (Gen. 12:1-3).

---

1. See a concordance for instances such as Matt. 17:21; Esther 4:16; Joel 1:14-20.

Abram believed. He went, and it was credited to him as righteousness. But 24 years later he still had not received a son. God appeared again, changed Abram's name to Abraham, and renewed his promise, saying, "Is anything too hard for the Lord?" (Gen. 18:14). Then, as a 99-year-old, and out of the discipline of silence, Abraham came boldly before the Lord. He pleaded for the preservation of Sodom and Gomorrah.

Often I have wondered, *If I had waited 24 years for something, would I have the courage to request something else?* I suspect that I should instead ask, "Out of the discipline of silence, what boldness in intercession does God want to give me?"

One year later Abraham received his son. To all of us for whom delay seems endless comes the promise, "They who wait for the Lord shall renew their strength, they shall mount up with wings like eagles, they shall run and not be weary, they shall walk and not faint" (Isa. 40:31 RSV).

Relinquishment

After waiting 25 years for a son, did Abraham clutch Isaac? The longer we pray for something, the more likely we are to come to that point where we, like Abraham, have to lay our "Isaac" on the altar.

Relinquishment means giving something totally to the Lord. We cannot hang on to it even in the tiniest little fiber of our being, for God knows.

Our two youngest have committed themselves to Christ's use of them through missions. For years I had worked as a mother does to protect these sons. Then one day our 19-year-old asked, "How would you feel about my going to Taiwan for a year to study Mandarin Chinese?"

Three days later the Spirit broke into my devotions with his persistent whisper: "Give up your Isaacs." I wondered why he used the plural form, but on my knees I prayed, "Lord, once again I give my sons to you—unconditionally and without reservation." A short time later, our 21-year-old told us he felt led

123

of God to transfer to a college with a major in missions, but half a continent away.

Relinquishment. For me it is never easy, and often it comes in stages. Later on, I realized I had gone beyond spiritual relinquishment to the emotional when I awakened with the prayer, "Thank you, Lord, that you have given them to us so that we *can* give them back to you."

Whether married or single, and no matter what the focus of our prayers, the more deeply we care about that for which we pray, the more likely we will need to come to relinquishment. The Spirit will show us the difference between wrestling as he leads and relinquishing.

Commitment

What counts in prayer is commitment to what God wants to do. Job described it well when he said, "Though he slay me, yet will I trust in him" (Job 13:15 KJV). It is our responsibility to pray, his to answer.

When our commitment to God's purpose enters deep into our being, it becomes an integral fiber in the fabric of our prayer life. We say with Paul, "I consider everything a loss compared to the surpassing greatness of knowing Christ Jesus my Lord" (Phil. 3:8). Or with the psalmist, "The nearness of God is my good" (73:28 NAS).

Not long ago I waited in a hospital room while my husband underwent tests because of the excruciating pain that was later found to be caused by a kidney stone. I had prayed. I had relinquished. Now I waited.

As the time grew long, I sensed once again the most important aspect of prayer—the relationship, the presence of Jesus Christ. Out of that he does his work in me.

I turned to Psalm 27 and read verses four and five over and over again until they entered deep into my being:

One thing I ask of the Lord,
    this is what I seek:
that I may dwell in the house of the Lord
    all the days of my life,
to gaze upon the beauty of the Lord
    and to seek him in his temple.
For in the day of trouble
    he will keep me safe in his dwelling;
he will hide me in the shelter of his
      tabernacle
    and set me high upon a rock.

14

The more difficult life is,
the greater our potential for joy—the joy
the Holy Spirit gives in spite
of circumstances.

Stand Up and Be Counted

As a child I chanted an old rhyme, "Sticks and stones may break my bones, but names and faces will never hurt me." Unknown to me, during that very time, Jews across the world were dying in Nazi Germany. For them persecution began with name-calling and snide remarks.

If we are aware of the times in which we live, you and I should hold no doubt about the extent of persecution worldwide. Often it begins slowly, insidiously, as sleeping giants fail to protest initial symptoms. People and nations take for granted that because they have had freedom in the past they always will. Yet behind the scenes, ruthless individuals maneuver their way into power. Like a snake coiling, preparing to strike, they wait only for that time when the bite is lethal. Then the poison spreads.

Is persecution a completely negative thing? Though none of us would welcome such suffering, historically speaking there have been some positive aspects. The early church stayed in Jerusalem until the persecution that broke out after Stephen's death. Everywhere they scattered, they preached the Word.

Persecuted people have always been alive people, filled with the fire of the Holy Spirit. Apathy, self-serving, and materialism vanish before necessary choices. Think of Christ's words as he described the end of the age:

> You will be handed over to be persecuted and put to death, and you will be hated by all nations because of me. At that time many will turn away from the faith and will betray and hate each other, and many false prophets will appear and deceive many people. Because of the increase of wickedness, the love of most will grow cold, but he who stands firm to the end will be saved. And this gospel of the kingdom will be preached in the whole world as a testimony to all nations, and then the end will come (Matt. 24:9-14).

In this passage, as well as in John 15:18-27, Jesus linked persecution with the spreading of the gospel. In such times we can expect a great outpouring of the Spirit in revival and missions. Those Christians who live and die in a way honoring to the Lord become, like martyred Stephen, the seed of the church.

If that is the case, do we desire the safe, secure way—even the way of betrayal—or the one in which we stand up to be counted? Let's consider some ideas garnered from the experiences of other Christians:

Past your fear

If our parents are conscientious, we learn from early childhood to please others. As we begin school, we find this attitude reinforced by teachers. When we want good grades, we "stay on their good side." Next comes peer pressure from our classmates; we must do as they do, and think as they think. And then? Then comes the time when our beliefs conflict with what others believe. Suddenly we are afraid.

A servant girl said to Peter, "You also were with Jesus of Galilee."

"I don't know what you're talking about," he answered. Twice more he denied Jesus. But consider the change after he was filled with the power of the Holy Spirit. When the highest officials of the church told Peter and John not to speak or teach in the name of Jesus, they stood in their faith: "Judge for yourselves whether it is right in God's sight to obey you rather than God. For we cannot help speaking about what we have seen and heard." Returning to the upper room, they prayed for boldness (Acts 4:19-20, 29-30).

For every Christian who desires to be used of God there comes a time of dealing with what people think. Always you and I need to be thoughtful about the feelings of others. But if we deny our beliefs in order to please someone, we place their opinion of us ahead of our allegiance to Jesus Christ.

I asked a group to which I spoke, "Are you willing to follow Jesus unconditionally and without reservation, even to the point of death if it should come to that?"

A young woman came forward, saying, "I always thought that was just part of my commitment as a Christian."

What you believe

Someone has said, "The best preparation for persecution is a prepared life." Jesus entered suffering having a special relationship with the Father. So, too, do we need a special relationship with the Father, Son, and Holy Spirit. Out of that we know without doubt what we believe.

We should also consider, "What is the most valuable possession I have?" It is not an option, but a necessity, that we nourish ourselves on Scripture. For that there is no substitute for memorization. I feel I do not truly know a verse or song until I wake up at night with the words going through my mind. Watchman Nee, a Chinese pastor imprisoned for 20 years, apparently never had a Bible in captivity, but lived on verses he had committed to memory.

Inscribed on Chet Bitterman's class ring were the words, "To know Him and To Make Him Known." A Wycliffe linguist, he memorized the entire book of 1 Peter, finding the verses on suffering especially meaningful. A short time later, Colombian terrorists captured Chet. After a 48-day ordeal, they murdered him. But only two days before the raid that imprisoned him,

Chet and his wife Brenda talked about increased guerilla activity. He said, "It's okay for someone to die for the sake of getting the Word of God to the minority people of Colombia."

Draw together

In moments of discouragement, whatever the cause, we desperately need one another. Today many are drawing together in Christian communities in order to help one another. Whether we do this or not, Christians should develop healthy working relationships, the old-fashioned trading of help and skills, and the ability to worship and pray together. As Leland Evenson said, "We need to say about one another, 'That's my brother—that's my sister,' out of a fellowship in which we are willing to lay down our lives for one another." If a group stays small and individuals know one another deeply, the probability of this happening increases.

Such groups should not be cliques, but rather places where we make disciples. Growing up in Korea, Dr. Paul Yonggi Cho experienced invasion first by the Japanese, then by the Communists. As pastor of Central Church, the world's largest local congregation, he holds a precarious position only a few miles from the North Korean border. He has divided his church into numerous small cell groups having weekly Bible study, prayer, and sharing of needs. Within these groups trust relationships have developed out of which they could give their lives for one another if necessary. The moment that Communists cross the border, congregational records will be destroyed, and cell groups will carry on the ministry of the church.

Division or loyalty?

When Billy Graham visited Russia, reporters quoted him as saying, "There is as much freedom here as in my hometown of Montreat, North Carolina." Christians asked one another: "Did you hear what Billy Graham said?" In a later statement, Dr. Graham cleared up the misunderstanding. Through the change of one word, "fervor," to "freedom," seeds of distrust were sown.

The problem points out something important—our desperate need for loyalty and a refusal to be divided. John Matthews, a pastor who traveled in Hungary, told a group:

> Governments can persecute a church, but they can never really destroy it. The most harmful things that can happen are what Christians do to each other. Some of the churches in Hungary were paralyzed because of the air of suspicion that was on the body of Christ. Our flesh breeds suspicion and the communists have learned to take advantage of it. If they get people afraid and suspicious of someone, it's easier to control society.

When Communists came into power in China, Watchman Nee's Shanghai congregation held out longer than most against demands to hold accusation meetings. At length and under extreme pressure, a meeting was called at which two representatives from the communist government addressed the church:

> Their speeches charging imperialism in the church's leaders brought only a bewildered silence. No one spoke in support. At length someone plucked up the courage to say: "Is it not true that Paul counted all things but loss for Christ? Should we not therefore count even our honoured People's Government the veriest refuse that we might gain Christ?" At this a cadre, planted in the meeting, burst out, "Watchman Nee ordered women to cover their heads in prayer. This is despotism!" Designed to be inflammatory, the charge merely backfired on the accuser. Brothers demanded who was this outsider who had put the question. (Angus I. Kinnear, *Against the Tide*, pp. 202-203).

At this important time, members remained loyal, refusing to denounce their pastor, Watchman Nee. The government continued to battle the congregation, but not with an outward demand to repudiate the name of Christ. That probably would have brought Christians together. Instead, the government attacked *the area they considered most vulnerable: the loyalty of Christians to one another.* Church members had to decide whether to believe in the integrity of certain Christians, Nee included. Often it was difficult to learn whether accusations were true.

Openness or honesty?

Inevitably the question comes, "If I became a political or religious prisoner, how would I react under questioning?" In its 1955 Code of Conduct for the Armed Forces, the United States instructs personnel to give only name, rank, service number, and date of birth if taken captive. Additional information can be used against our country or the prisoner. Interrogators often try to break the spirit of prisoners by describing untrue deaths of a wife, mother, or loved one.

Remaining silent poses a problem for Christians who believe that through their witness a person may come to know Jesus Christ. In normal times what seems to be persecution can be a questioning that eventually leads a person to faith. For that kind of seeking, we should "always be prepared to give an answer to everyone who asks you to give the reason for the hope that you have" (1 Peter 3:15). But persecutors often pretend to seek Christ in order to gain incriminating evidence. I can think of no way to know the difference except through the discernment of the Lord and absolute, unflinching dependence on him.

Christians also need to understand the difference between openness and honesty. We are called to be honest; we are not expected to be open under every circumstance. In time of persecution this applies to conversations with both enemies and friends. During World War II, French Christians under Nazi occupation needed to know enough to work together, yet so little that they could not be forced to betray one another. They could not tell what they did not know.

During his trial, Jesus remained silent much of the time, apparently speaking only when led by the Holy Spirit. Thinking about this, I remembered a time when I desperately needed to grow in the Lord, and spent half an hour telling a person all the things I felt wrong about the way he believed.

131

When I finished, he did not defend himself. His beliefs were scriptural, and he felt no need to argue his position.

Seeing this, I thought, *There has to be something here I haven't grasped.* Within 24 hours God worked so powerfully in my spirit that I went to that individual and asked forgiveness for what I had said.

As God's people, have we even begun to grasp what it means to *not* speak if led by the Holy Spirit? Did Christ's silence bring the officials and officers of the guard to a later faith?

During a time of high unemployment, a college student named Jim inquired or left his application for summer employment at more than 30 places. Then one day he gained a new insight into Christ's promise to his disciples: "Whenever you are arrested and brought to trial, do not worry beforehand about what to say. Just say whatever is given you at the time, for it is not you speaking, but the Holy Spirit" (Mark 13:11).

As Jim waited for an interview at a pizza house, a question popped into his mind: "What makes you think you're qualified for this job?" Never had he been asked that question, but immediately the Holy Spirit gave the answer. Moments later he was called in, and the interviewer used the exact words the Spirit had given: "What makes you think you're qualified for this job?"

"My Christian faith and experience," Jim answered. He told about his short-term missionary experience, and how he had witnessed on the streets of New Orleans during Mardi Gras. Referring to the perverted, carnival atmosphere, he said, "I mingled with all kinds of people, but even when it was really hard, God enabled me to keep my cool."

He did not acquire the job, but received the deep satisfaction of knowing he had been used by God.

Revenge or hope?

T. Simon Farisani, a South African pastor who has been cruelly tortured many times, said this: "The more you suffer, the more difficult it is to hate."

David knew that. Forced to flee as his son Absalom connived for his throne, David met two kinds of treatment. From a servant named Ziba came donkeys, bread, raisin cakes, figs, and wine. From Shimei, a member of Saul's clan, spewed forth cursing. David experienced, as you may have, that when we are down, some amaze us by their kindness. Others kick us (2 Sam. 16:1-14). Very simply David said, "It may be that the Lord will see my distress and repay me with good for the cursing I am receiving today" (v. 12). Hundreds of years later, Christ said, "Pray for those who persecute you," and "great is your reward in heaven" (Matt 5:44, 12).

In his book *When Bad Things Happen to Good People,* Rabbi Harold Kushner cites German theologian Dorothee Sölle. In her book *Suffering,* she suggests that "the most important question we can ask about suffering is whom it serves. Does our suffering serve God or the devil, the cause of becoming alive or being morally paralyzed?"

Kushner explains the difference: Our faith is strengthened by the death of some who died in a way that bore witness to their faith. Those are God's martyrs. But if we react to someone's death with a despair that is a loss of faith, we make such persons the devil's martyrs (p. 137).

The more difficult life is, the greater our potential for joy. Not the surface kind of happiness that comes only when things go well; instead, we receive the joy that the Holy Spirit gives in spite of circumstances.

One Sunday morning, as we sang the opening hymn at our church, I received a vision that should have discouraged me, but instead offered hope. I saw an individual tied to a cross-like stake. As flames shot upward, the person began singing, and I sensed that deeply-felt quality in which lungs expand and every word is dedicated to the Lord. The higher the flames, the more fervently the person sang from the depths of a freed spirit.

Soon it was time for the special music, and triumphant words flowed through a male vocalist: "I have tasted a freedom, I can go where he's leading, the shackles will hold me no more. . . . This is the time I must sing. . . ." [2]

Later, during the closing hymn, I once again saw the person at the stake, standing firm. Again the flames shot upward, and there came that heartfelt singing from the depths of a totally committed spirit. There was no mistaking the victory.

As I prayed about what I had seen, I sensed it would be the kind of world into which I would go. Each person unconditionally committed to follow Jesus Christ will enter that same world. We cannot accept any cross lightly, whether it be death to selfish desires or death to life. But what is our hope?

In *Bridges to Hope*, Alvin Rogness tells how a Nazi interrogator repeatedly tried to break Hans Lilje, a German pastor and later bishop of Hannover. After threatening him with death, the official sat speechless because of Lilje's calm reply: "But I don't need to live."

Whatever comes to us, you and I hold that undeniable victory.

---

2. From "This Is the Time I Must Sing," by William J. and Gloria Gaither. © Copyright 1975 by William J. Gaither/ASCAP. All rights reserved. International copyright secured. Used by permission of The Benson Company, Inc., Nashville.

15

An effective ministry is not thrown together haphazardly. It develops according to God's plan and our acceptance of his progression.

Effective Kingdom Ministry

His neatly trimmed beard emphasized the strong lines of his face. At 21, he thinks often about life: "All of us were pulled out of nothing," he said. "It's not just our bodies that are so amazing. Each of us has an individual personality and character."

He grinned. "It's a privilege to live! I have to ask, 'Why was I created?' I know Christ's overall purpose is to draw all people unto himself. But why was it necessary for *me* to be born? I can't help but think there's something specific God wants me to do."

Long ago, when Jesus saw the crowds, "he had compassion for them, because they were harassed and helpless, like sheep without a shepherd." To his disciples he said, "The harvest is plentiful, but the laborers are few; pray therefore the Lord of the harvest to send out laborers into his harvest" (Matt. 9:36-38 RSV).

We are those laborers. Is there something God wants us to do? Could it be that he desires your life and mine to leave a

135

specific imprint on this world? Yet how often do we seem torn in every direction, weighed down by the tyranny of the urgent? Do we lack even the power to serve?

God brings our lives together out of his great love for us. Yet with that gift we accept responsibility—his use of us. Often we forget that the Lord shows us his faithfulness that we may in turn encourage the wholeness of others. He needs laborers—not persons running in every direction, but individuals freed by knowing their full potential in Christ Jesus. Let's consider seven steps through which God releases us into effective kingdom ministry:

Know your ministry

The word "ministry" refers to *the particular way in which we serve God by serving others.* Whoever we are and whatever our age, each of us has a potential ministry. For some, daily work and ministry are one. For others, the two are separate. Whether we brown-bag it or enter an executive office, God can use us. When we remember that, our daily tasks and our ministry tend to blend more and more.

To be set free in ministry, we need to sense the specific way in which God calls us. Some individuals receive a deep and unmistakable experience in which they know without doubt God's will for their life. Others drift gradually into a situation and suddenly realize God is using them. Or a class assignment pushes them into choosing a vocation, and they discover they want to learn more. Still others respect someone in a particular ministry and desire to enter that field of service. Or they have the feeling, "That's right for me. I enjoy it."

If you are unsure about your ministry, seek the will of God. Ask him, "Lord, reveal the area in which you want to use me. Give me a sense of being called." Often we recognize our call when the desire to work in a certain area comes upon us so strongly that we cannot refuse it. Other times we simply sense peace as we study or do those things necessary to serve.

Establish priorities

While working in a short-term missionary program, one youth discovered a secret of ministry: "If you know God as he really is, you can't help but trust him. If you trust him, you can't help but love him. Out of love flows obedient service."

Too many people enter Christian service with minimal commitment, wanting the best of both worlds. We need to ask, "Whose work is it, mine or the Lord's?" If you believe it is yours, you have not received his call.

At times most of us feel overwhelmed by the tremendous needs of the world. In those moments it helps to see ministry as part of a life pattern by asking, "What can I do that no one else can do?"

Whether we are male or female, God establishes priorities for each of us. If married, we should be concerned about God first, our marriage partner second, our children third, and service outside the home fourth. When I was young, my mother once said, "If we fail with you children, nothing else matters." I am deeply grateful that her ministry during our growing-up years was our home.

For a single person without children, it is less complicated: God first, service second. But whether we are single or married, the Lord's priorities do not give us permission to neglect any area. The more responsibilities we have, the more vulnerable we are to tension in working out our different responsibilities. That's where the power of the Holy Spirit is especially helpful.

In all things, we need to face Jesus at every turn, being cautious how we build: "For no one can lay any foundation other than the one already laid, which is Jesus Christ. If any man builds on this foundation using gold, silver, costly stones, wood, hay or straw, his work will be shown for what it is, because the Day will bring it to light. It will be revealed with fire, and the fire will test the quality of each man's work" (1 Cor. 3:11-13).

Live in God's power

Paul warned Timothy that in the last days there would be those having the form of godliness, but denying its power (2 Tim. 3:5). As Christians, we have the Holy Spirit within us, but we cannot be effective in ministry unless we live in his power. That's the reason for Pentecost. Jesus knew his disciples were not adequately equipped without the propulsion of the Holy Spirit.

If you lack the power needed for ministry, ask forgiveness for sin. If you have been involved in any area of the occult, including the reading of horoscopes, name it specifically, praying, "I renounce any occult involvement, any unholy spirit." Then ask, "Jesus, release in me all the power of your Holy Spirit, that I may be a more effective witness for you." Receive that power in faith, thanking God for it. Later, if you experience difficult times and sense you need additional help, ask Jesus for a fresh filling of his Spirit and the incomparable power described by Paul (see Eph. 1:17-21).

Foundational to God's service should be our belief in the divine inspiration and authority of the Bible. God's Word offers a resource and power base out of which we help others. Warren Wiersbe writes:

> The men and women of faith who are enshrined in Hebrews 11 were ordinary people who accomplished extraordinary things simply because they trusted God's Word. They made mistakes. (The people who don't make mistakes don't make anything. They are spectators and critics, not pioneers.) They even sinned against the Lord. But the total impact of their lives was one of faith in God. Some were delivered by faith; others suffered and died by faith. Either way, they trusted God and He was glorified.

Athletes pay a price for the training that undergirds a winning game. When we think of their commitment, we need to ask, "Do I live in spiritual discipline? Through the power of the Holy Spirit, do I form good habits, concentrate, and work at those things that strengthen God's use of me? As Oswald

Chambers said, "My worth to God in public is what I am in private" (*My Utmost for His Highest*, p. 77).

Evaluate your attitudes

In *The Release of the Spirit*, Watchman Nee makes an important point: "Anyone who serves God will discover sooner or later that the great hindrance to his work is not others but himself" (p. 9). Problems with pride offer a good example: we think we don't need to learn, we refuse instruction, or we feel we deserve a place of honor and public applause.

Often pride takes a form we don't recognize as quickly, because it disguises itself as humility. When we struggle with a fear of failure or feelings of worthlessness, we can't do anything right. That means, of course, we can't do anything at all. Our need for excessive approval thwarts God's use of us. One of my sons calls it "pride of the worm."

If you and I are to be fully used in ministry, we need God-given self-esteem out of which we help others without demanding attention for our own interests. That does not mean we should continually live without having our personal needs met. But in balanced humility we recognize that God takes care of our interests if we take care of his.

In everything he did, Jesus sought his Father's honor, not his own, saying, "If I glorify myself, my glory means nothing" (John 8:54). A. W. Tozer writes in *The Pursuit of God*, "The whole course of the life is upset by failure to put God where He belongs. We exalt ourselves instead of God and the curse follows" (p. 107).

Each of us needs to make a once-for-all decision to glorify Jesus above all else. With each new test of our ego, we choose again. Whether we experience success or failure, we have the opportunity to lift Jesus higher.

At the base of all these attitudes should lie our willingness to live in repentance. To be fully used by God in ministry, we must first kneel before the cross. We cannot help someone else recognize sin as sin unless we have done so ourselves. God will use us in direct proportion to how often we return to that cross.

Become a servant

Jesus said, "Whoever wants to become great among you must be your servant, and whoever wants to be first must be your slave—just as the Son of Man did not come to be served, but to serve, and to give his life as a ransom for many" (Matt. 20:26-28). One perceptive young adult described it this way: "The better known you are as a leader, the more you have to be a servant."

During his last night with his disciples, Jesus washed their feet, saying, "I have set you an example that you should do as I have done for you" (John 13:15). Earlier he encouraged service in the most distasteful way possible. When Roman soldiers passed through a town, they required its inhabitants to carry baggage for a mile beyond. But Jesus said, " 'If someone forces you to go one mile, go with him two miles' " (Matt. 5:41). What was the difference between the first mile and the second? *The willingness to do more than required,* not to advance themselves, but to help another.

Servanthood involves sacrifice: getting out of bed to give a child a cup of cold water; putting aside convenience for the comfort of others; listening for unspoken cries that are shouts of anguish. To be a servant is to be Christ-like. No job is beneath us, unless it is contrary to his holiness.

Yet when we serve people, we do so for their betterment, not their detriment. Being a servant does not mean allowing people to continually waste our time because they want a problem instead of wholeness. The Lord desires to use us for honest needs. That's the difference between a servant and a doormat.

Think of a mother who picks up towels from the bathroom floor instead of teaching her children to do so. Or a father who lets his teenagers take the family car without expecting them to fill its tank now and then. Both are doormats because they fail to encourage responsibility. If we are servants in the image of Christ, we guide, comfort, encourage, and correct those whom the Lord gives us, inspiring them to reach their best.

Jesus showed us the difference between performance and ministry. Consider Abraham Lincoln, Martin Luther King Jr., and Mother Teresa. God uses those willing to serve the helpless or downtrodden. They refuse to elevate themselves, and the fruit of their servanthood elevates them for us.

Discern spiritual harassment

Satan delights in harassing those whose work threatens his own. In what better way can he ruin an effective ministry than through marital unfaithfulness? Another often-used tool is confusion.

A vital part of our preparation for ministry is the process of stripping away the selfishness that would interfere with God's work through us. As Paul described it: "Your attitude should be the same as that of Christ Jesus: Who, being in very nature God, did not consider equality with God something to be grasped, but made himself nothing, taking the very nature of a servant . . ." (Phil. 2:5-7). Yet too often Satan confuses our need to die to selfish desires with feelings of worthlessness. Think of it like this:

Dying to selfish desires:
Enabler: Holy Spirit
Purpose: to remove pride and other hindrances to ministry
Result: freedom, joy in work, productivity, reaching full potential in Jesus Christ.

Feelings of worthlessness:
Enabler: Satan
Purpose: to keep us from effective work
Result: concentration on self and feelings of condemnation, little or no output, being less than what God intends for us to be.

In this connection, the Holy Spirit made me aware of two passages. The first, Matthew 25:24-29, reveals the master's anger at the servant who did not use his talents to his full capability. In the second, Acts 13:46, Paul said to a group of Jews:

"We had to speak the word of God to you first. Since you reject it and *do not consider yourselves worthy of eternal life,* we now turn to the Gentiles." If we do not consider ourselves worthy of salvation, we won't receive it. In the same way, if we do not think ourselves worthy of God's help in our daily work, we cut ourselves off from it.

Accept in faith God's plan and timing

An effective ministry is not thrown together haphazardly. It develops according to the Lord's plan and our acceptance of his progression. Sometimes he allows what appears to be a slump for our growth in ministry. We may need experience in walking by faith, instead of feelings.

One of the greatest reasons for unrest in God's service is a failure to wait for his timing. We receive his call, even some experience within that call. We're on the countdown for lift-off. Then everything goes on hold. For months, and sometimes years, nothing gets off the ground. God is silent. Yet if we listen, we discover his silence is a way of speaking.

Alan Langstaff says, "I have seen more ministries miss their calling because they have tried to pressure cook things, than in any other way. God will often allow things to simmer for some time before they are ready to come to the boil."

Through a dream, Jacob's son Joseph caught a glimpse of how God would use him. His responsibilities as a prisoner prepared him to administrate immeasurable quantities of grain. Or think of Moses. Reared in a palace, he received his call as he looked on the burden of his people. Trying to take things into his own hands, he murdered an Egyptian, and God sent him into Midian for 40 years. There he became "the most humble man in all the earth," equipped to lead the greatest exodus in history.

God repeats that pattern often—even with his own Son. In the desert Christ faced temptations uniquely tailored to destroy his life's work. When he refuted those temptations with Scripture, he allowed God to turn them into tests that strengthened him for ministry.

Whatever form our time of waiting takes, God uses it to work in the character traits needed for service. Strengthening our commitment to him, and to the way he chooses to use us, he asks, "Are you ready to follow me unconditionally and without reservation?" Always he desires a quality in our lives expressed in the prayer of Peter Marshall, son of the Senate chaplain: "Lord, hide me behind yourself that you may be seen and heard, and not just me."

First the call, then the period of waiting, then a release into a new level of ministry, for which God has painstakingly prepared us. As we minister to others, seeing God's blessing in a situation, we receive greater faith for dealing with our own circumstances. Reasons for falling apart become evidence of God's faithfulness in helping us come together.

So, too, with Eric Liddle, the Olympic gold medal winner whose refusal to run on Sunday caught the attention of the world. Portrayed in the Academy award-winning *Chariots of Fire* and the book *The Flying Scotsman* by Sally Magnusson, Liddle had a strange running style. Ian Charleston, who played Eric, had a difficult time learning to run that way. Then one day, in a flash of insight, he realized it was like one of the trust exercises he had known in drama school: "He ran with faith. He didn't even look where he was going."

Eric literally trusted that he would get there. The moment he threw his head back was the moment he found something extra. When asked the secret of his success, he said, "The first half I run as fast as I can, and the second half I run faster with God's help."

When he became a missionary, he lived as he had trained to run. He became one with the Chinese in hardship, privation, and danger, ministering to them with great courage. When war came, he did not waste his last years, though spent in a prison camp, separated from his wife, and never seeing the youngest of his three children. Turning even his prison experience into a creative opportunity for the kingdom, Eric died with the words, "It's complete surrender."

The fields are white unto harvest. God needs laborers with an understanding of the times and an unconditional willingness to serve. "Always give yourselves fully to the work of the Lord," says Paul, "because you know that your labor in the Lord is not in vain" (1 Cor. 15:58).

That is the victory! To the faithful God shows himself faithful. Through the power of the Holy Spirit we, too, can live in a way that proclaims, "It's surrender—complete surrender!"